Ireland's Sea Fisheries: a History

Ireland's Sea Fisheries: a History

John de Courcy Ireland

The Glendale Press
DUBLIN

ISBN 0 907606 01 6

The Glendale Press
18 Sharavogue
Glenageary Road Upper,
Dun Laoghaire, Co. Dublin

Contents

Dedication

This book is dedicated to the fishermen of Ireland, past, present and to come, from every port from Donegal and Antrim to Kerry and Cork. e a queste persone che sono state l'ispirazione di una vita di lotta per la creazione di una vera economia marittima irlandese – B., V., V., T., K–J., il colonello L., il capitano K.

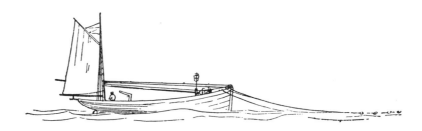

Acknowledgements

I would like to thank Mr. Patrick Flood of the Irish Commission on Maritime History for his patient discovery of documents referring to the Irish fishing industry in the last century, Mr. Peter Pearson of the Maritime Institute of Ireland for valuable information, Mr. John Wright of B.I.M. for provision of much documentation, Miss Mary Redahan for successfully typing what must have seemed an illegible manuscript, and my grandson Solomon MacEoghan for having arranged all my documentation in such meticulous chronological order.

Grateful acknowledgement is also due to the following sources: for supplying photographic material — National Museum of Ireland pp. 10, 36, 42, 64, 65, 69, 73, 87, 88, 90, 104, 105, 106, 113 and 114; National Library of Ireland pp. 15, 51, 57, 58, 59, 61, 74, 75, 77, 79, 82, 86, 89 and 94; Lambeth Palace Library p. 21; Science Museum, London (Crown copyright) pp. 23, 38 and 39, (Photo) p. 37; Rijksmuseum (Nederlands Scheepvaart Museum) p. 26; Trinity College Library (Molyneux Papers) p. 32; H.M. Stationery Office, Public Record Office (Crown copyright) pp. 33-5; Gillman Marine Collection pp. 45 and 50; State Paper Office p. 84; The National Maritime Museum p. 91; University College, Dublin, Department of Folklore pp. 102 and 103; The Irish Skipper Journal pp. 108, 116, 118, 128(top), 131, 152, 154, 158, and 178; Bord Iascaigh Mhara pp. 110, 111, 115, 119, 123, 129, 132, 133, 135, 137, 139, 140, 144, 145 (bottom), 147, 148, 150, 151, 155, 159, 160, 161, 163, 164, 166, 167, 168, 171, 172 and 173; Bord Fáilte p 128 (bottom); George Morrison p. 145 (top); Fisheries Research Laboratory, Coleraine p. 142; to the Department of Agriculture for Northern Ireland (Fisheries Division) for statistical information; to Hal Sisk for aiding with photographic identification and to Arthur Reynolds of the *Irish Skipper Journal.*

J. DE COURCY IRELAND
1981

1

Introduction

We have always had a vigorous sea-going tradition in Ireland. We Irish are a mixed people of varied origins, of which every section inevitably arrived by sea. The earliest settlers, who braved the storms and currents of the North Channel and settled along the Antrim coast were certainly fishermen, as is shown by the contents of midden heaps they left behind. Archaeological research shows that Mesolithic, Neolithic, Copper, Bronze and early Iron Age Irish were in touch by sea with communities in other lands. The "Story-Lore of the Leinstermen", ("probably written down in the ninth century, it is one of the best told old Irish tales that have been preserved", according to Dr. M.A. O'Brien in a 1953 Thomas Davis lecture) has as hero Labraidh Loingsech, "Labraidh the Seafarer". Lecturing in 1973 to Ollscoil Bhaile Atha Cliath, Professor James Carney of the Institute of Advanced Studies referred to "the earliest poem of any length that survived from the purely native tradition", written probably before the year 500 to a south Leinster prince called Nad Buidh, in which "the Irish were presented as a seafaring people". Irish seamen who helped finish off the dying Roman Empire, and their descendants who carried out the remarkable Atlantic voyages echoes of which have come down to us in the Brendan legend, were surely not

ignorant of the art of sea-fishing. Eoin MacNeill in his master-piece on early Irish laws and institutions showed that fishermen had a recognized status in early Irish society. Certainly the Norsemen, who made up a fair proportion of the ancestry of our present population, knew a great deal about sea fishing, and the words in Irish of several types of fish and of boats, for fishing-line and other nautical terms are of Norse origin. We know, moreover, from their own sagas that Norsemen were accompanied on many of their distant voyages by Gaelic speaking Irish. Al-Qazwini, one of the great Arab medieval geographers, quoting the scholar Al-'Udhri (1002—1085), a luminary of Moorish Spain, recorded the existence of a whale fishery off our south coast. Age-old traditions of cod fishing west of the Aran Islands were recalled by the 17th century west of Ireland chronicler Roderick O'Flaherty.

Ireland in the Middle Ages possessed many flourishing ports — the sixteenth-century chronicler, Holinshed, gave the number as eighty-eight in his time. Ships built, manned and owned in Ireland were trading regularly with Bordeaux across the tempestuous Bay of Biscay in the fourteenth century, and in the fifteenth century there were years when Chester, then the leading English port for trade with the northern

A boat made in gold found at Broighter, Co. Derry, dated the first century AD, and now in the National Museum, Dublin. Measuring 18.5 cm in length, this is a model of a ship "clearly in the skin-boat tradition, and, therefore, ancestral to the modern large currach" (Prof. E. G. Bowen in Britain and the Western Seaways *p. 187)*

half of Ireland, saw more Irish-owned ships along her quays than ships from England itself or any other country. By the fifteenth century the Irish sea fisheries were famous throughout western Europe and greedily coveted by foreigners but, as I shall show below, had long, despite many difficulties, been worked by Irish fishermen as well as Englishmen, Welshmen, French-men, Bretons, Spaniards and other continentals.

The political upheavals of the second half of the sixteenth century led to a decline in maritime activities in Ireland, yet the seventeenth century saw not only Irish seamen making a name for themselves under foreign flags, but also, towards the end of it, a revival of ship-owning and ship-building in our ports.

John Philip Holland, in the conning tower of his submarine, April 1898, New Jersey. Born in Clare, he became a teacher. A coast guard's son, he was always interested in the sea, and after emigrating to the United States he became one of the leading world pioneers of submarine navigation.

The eighteenth century, so long dismissed in the history text-books as a period of unmitigated doom and gloom, proves the remarkable resilience of the Irish people and the tenacity of their maritime traditions. Not only did Irish seamen in Irish-owned ships defy all the difficulties of the time and trade successfully in the Mediterranean and across the Atlantic, not only did Irishmen serve with distinction in the navies of France, Spain, Portugal, Britain, the Austrian Empire, the newly-founded United States, Russia and some of the states of divided Italy, but ship-building also flourished at home and so did the fishing industry, for brief periods.

In the nineteenth century, more people were fishing at sea from our shores than ever before or since, but at a very low productive level. It was an Irish-owned ship with an Irish crew which in 1836 made the first ever voyage under steam across the Atlantic from east to west. It was the Irish-owned and largely Irish-manned ships of the City of Dublin Steam Packet Company which at various points in the century were the world's fastest ships and were the pioneers of the many short-sea passenger services booming in Europe today. Early in that century Dublin Bay saw the establishment of Europe's first organised lifeboat service, manned largely by fishermen. Our island produced two of the greatest marine engineers of all time — John Philip

The Hon. Charles Parsons from Birr, Co. Offaly, one of the greatest marine engineers of all time. He died in 1931.

Holland, the submarine pioneer, and Charles Algernon Parsons, the perfector of the marine steam turbine. Ireland was building ships for many countries, as she continued to do ever since. Thomas Davis, the Young Irelander, foretold a great future for our maritime economy.

But from the middle of the last century onwards the intelligenzia of Ireland began to display our own particular Irish version of what the French writer, Julien Benda, called 'la trahison des clercs' — the treason of the educated. They turned their backs on the sea by and large, banished all memory of our maritime traditions from the schools, the educational text books and the universities, and preached an inward-looking, introverted philosophy. The result was that, when war broke out in 1939 and threatened the independence we had so hardly won, we had no navy to protect our shores and trade, an insignificant fishing industry in a state of rapid decay, and only a tiny handful of ships — not more than 40,000 tons of shipping in all — to handle vital imports and exports.

It has been a long haul back to sanity from those disastrous days, and we still have a long way to go to develop our maritime potential to the limits demanded by practical visionaries in our past like Swift, Davis, and Arthur Griffith — the only one of the founding fathers of the Irish state of today who actively advocated the development of our sea fisheries. The state owns two flourishing shipping concerns, the shipowners of Arklow are still in business, and a few small ships are being successfully operated by other private owners. This island nation, however, is still only sixty-fourth in the table of shipowning countries,

Fishing with nets, reproduced in Gilbert, Facsimiles of the National Manuscripts of Ireland, Vol. IV

with a smaller merchant fleet than landlocked Switzerland. We have now an efficient naval service with four modern ships and more promised, but it is still too small for the tasks imposed on it and remains the cinderella of the three defence forces. Our fisheries have been developed as never before in the past decade and a half, and we are consuming more fish per head, more intelligently prepared, than ever in the past. But there remains an ocean of tasks to make our fishing industry second to none in the European Economic Community in the realms of productivity, training, safety and above all research. And, if ship-building and boat-building are still far from dead in Ireland, as a people utterly dependent on the seas around us we are still too indifferent to their possibilities and their importance.

2

Ireland's Sea Fisheries in the Middle Ages

Burke's *Industrial History of Ireland,* published in 1933, gave a clearer picture of Ireland's past than most Leaving Certificate history textbooks till quite recently and clearer, indeed, than many allegedly weightier studies. Burke wrote (p. 17):

> From the thirteenth century onwards the Irish fisheries assume an increasing importance. That fish had become definitely an article of trade in Ireland at this period is seen from a study of the Charters granted to the various Irish towns by the English kings. Herrings, salmon, and fish in general are included in the items upon which the citizens of places like Dublin, Drogheda, and Youghal are entitled to raise taxes for the maintenance of their fortifications. An Italian map of Ireland in 1339 reveals the existence of three fishing banks off the coast of Wicklow, while at the opening of the sixteenth century, when Irish fisheries had attracted the attention of continental powers, another Italian map shows three fishing banks off Arklow, one outside Dublin and two in the vicinity of Ardglass in County Down. As early as 1437 salmon and herrings are found in the list of Irish exports, notably to Brabant (modern Belgium).

George O'Brien, long revered as modern Ireland's leading economic historian,

wrote in *The Economic History of Ireland in the Seventeenth Century* (p. 80):

> The greater part of the fishing carried on in the seas adjoining Ireland was in the hands of foreigners, with whom the Irish made little or no attempt to compete. From a very early time foreign fishermen had been accustomed to fish in Irish waters.

O'Brien's view is repeated in a more recent work, Kenneth Nicholl's *Gaelic and Gaelicised Ireland in the Middle Ages* (p. 120):

> The fisheries carried on off the southern and western coasts of Ireland were of great economic importance during the late medieval period, and brought in a large revenue to the lords of the adjacent coasts in the form of fishing dues, charges for the use of harbours and of drying grounds for nets and for the fish itself, etc. The fishery itself, however, was always carried on by foreign vessels, although Irish merchants might on occasions have a stake in it. In 1534 some merchants of Dingle contracted with a Breton sea-captain at Bordeaux to ship twenty tons of wine . . . to Ireland; the cargo discharged, the vessel was to take on extra hands [these would surely have been Irish

A Portolan chart. From about 1300 AD the Italians and Catalans produced great numbers of practical sea charts of the European and Mediterranean coastlines. These were known as portolans as they plotted their way from port to port. In 1513 an edition of Ptolemy's world map, published in Strasbourg, included a number of modern maps, among them a woodcut of the British Isles by Martin Waldseemüller, from which Ireland is here reproduced. This is a version of a type of portolan map characterised by a large Clew Bay filled with islands. Many of the placenames have been identified

fishermen; J. deC.I.] and engage in fishing off the Irish coast. The fisheries off Hook Head in the south-east, those centred on Baltimore in the south-west and the herring fishery off Aran Island in County Donegal are noted as being especially valuable.

At least one expert much more closely associated with twentieth-century Irish fishing than any of these writers has also opined that the country's rich grasslands and general fertility militated against the development of any significant Irish fishing industry at any rate before the late eighteenth-century.

Foreigners undoubtedly fished profitably off our coasts from early in the Middle Ages. Nevertheless, just as there is proof that Irish-owned and Irish-manned merchant ships were active on the trade routes of north-west Europe from the fourteenth century on, so also is there evidence that by no means all the fish caught in Irish waters in those days was caught by foreigners. Documents preserved in England clearly show that armies of Kings Edward I and II campaigning in Scotland in the thirteenth and early fourteenth centuries depended a considerable amount on dried fish received from Ireland for their food supplies. It is hardly likely that those fish had been caught and cured by anybody but Irish fishermen.

The local customs account for the English port of Chester for the year 1404—5 has a large number of entries referring to the importation in Irish ships by Irish merchants of herring, red herring, white fish, salmon, dry fish and just 'fish'. What is more significant still, many of these Irish ships carried back home salt for the preservation of fish (Chester lies close to England's largest salt mines). It would take a considerable effort of the imagination to suppose that these Irish merchants

and ship-masters were bringing to England fish caught by Englishmen and taking salt back to Ireland for packing herrings caught here by resident English fishermen. Among the Chester customs entries for 1404—5 are the following:

23 October 1404:
outward custom on a cart of salt for a Drogheda merchant.

24 October 1404:
inward custom paid by no fewer than eight Drogheda men on herrings they were importing, six of whom took salt away with them (nine horseloads of it in one case, two carts and four horse-loads in another, testimony, one would think, to considerable fishing activity off the Boyne Estuary).

27 October 1404:
also from Drogheda, customs paid by a Drogheda man on three barrels of herring.

7 December 1404:
two Rush men paid dues on one 'pipe' and two 'mease' of red herring they had brought in.

20 December 1404:
a Dublin shipmaster paid dues on herring imported and salt shipped out by him.

28 January 1405:
Richard de Newton and Thomas Rede of Malahide each imported one 'last' of herring.

26 March 1405:
Richard Coyne of Rush and John Drakesspere of Drogheda paid dues on white fish imported.

April 1405:
men from Balrothery, Rush, Drogheda (John Macouw) and Malahide brought in white fish, others herring (Dublin and Malahide men), and Dublin men Eustace and Walsh paid export dues on salt, though this is not specifically stated to be for preserving herring.

IRELAND – MAIN FISHING PORTS IN THE FIFTEENTH AND SIXTEENTH CENTURIES

Fishing ports ●

Ports without urban development *Berehaven*

Lough Foyle

The Bann

Aran

Killybegs

Rafran and Moy Estuary *Assaroe*

Ardglass

Sligo

Drogheda

Galway

Dublin Malahide

Aran Islands

Wicklow

Arklow

Wexford

Waterford

Dingle

Dungarvan

Youghal

Hook Head

Dunmore East

Kinsale

Berehaven

Baltimore

July 1405:

Richard Coyne of Rush was back with 'fish' and so was his fellow townsman, John Roos.

September 1405:

Rush men imported white fish and salmon and Malahide men herring, and exported salt.

In the fifteenth-century port records for Bristol, then England's second city, we find a Drogheda merchant arriving with salmon, merchants from Waterford settled locally and engaged in importing fish from off our southern coasts, and Irishmen called Gough and Lawless who were masters of Bristol-owned ships (are we to suppose that two such men knew nothing of sea fishing?).

Eileen Power and M.M. Postan, in their *Studies in English Trade in the Fifteenth Century*, remark that 'fish was probably the product of Ireland that Bristol men valued most'. Moreover, 'they chaffered for it in Ireland with fishermen, who sometimes promised to send it at least as far as Kingrode' (near the mouth of the Bristol Avon), which suggests that the Irish had quite a considerable hold over their own fisheries at that time. Moreover, these authors quote the case of a Malahide fisherman, John Mold, who provided a Bristol merchant with fish for export to Spain, and 'a Lusk fisherman's wife who possessed (besides sheep, cows, pigs and a cart horse) one boat and fourteen sea-nets'. And what about Thomas Hanyagh of Kinsale (associated with other Kinsale shipmasters named Martyn and Galway) who, some weeks after being involved in a piratical act off the south coast of Ireland, 'turned up in Bristol with a skiff of Kinsale and 6,000 hake' (a fairly recently discovered luxury) belonging to other Kinsale merchants?

Power and Postan also quote the arrival from Ireland in fifteenth-century Bristol of 'pecys of saltfisch', pollack, cod, whiting and ling. They mention the continuous arrival in the English port of ships owned in Waterford, Ross, Youghal and Limerick as well as the other Irish ports mentioned before, and emphasise once again that fish was a favourite import from this country, and salt an important export from Bristol to Ireland for the sake of salting fish caught in Irish waters. They allude also to the regular participation of Irish ships in England's flourishing fifteenth-century trade with Iceland. These ships went to Iceland to load fish for England. The authors do not mention Irishmen fishing in the Icelandic fishing grounds; Englishmen did, however, and it seems not at all impossible that Irishmen followed suit. After all, Irish seamen had been familiar with Icelandic waters ever since the days of the saintly scholars, long before any Englishman sailed there.

The evidence of Power and Postan is strengthened by the researches of Professor H. Touchard, in his monumental *Le Commerce Maritime Breton à la Fin du Moyen Age*. He refers in particular to three Irish ships as early as 1383 at Le Collet in the extreme south of Brittany picking up salt for curing herring at home.

Alice Stopford Green, in her thoroughly documented *The Making of Ireland and its Undoing*, mentions her discovery that Breton salt was exported to the Donegal O'Donnells for their herring fishery — no suggestion that the O'Donnells had ceded the whole of their herring fishery to foreigners, though there is no doubt that part of it was rented out. She also cites the example of fishermen from Duncannon and Waterford carrying their hake to France, and MacSweeneys, O'Briens and O'Malleys fishing 'their own seas'. Moreover, she writes of Irish ships exporting Irish fish to Bruges in Flanders as far back as the early fourteenth century.

James Lydon, in his *Ireland in the Later Middle Ages* (Gill and Macmillan 1973), referring to the household accounts of the prior of Holy Trinity, Dublin, in the late thirteenth century, states that: 'In Lent and on Fridays, plenty of fish was available: salmon, oysters, salted fish and herring were the most common; less (does he mean *more*?) rarely, for special guests, trout, eels, turbot, plaice, gurnard and salted eels were on the menu.' It is self-evident that these fish must have been caught by local fishermen. Lydon refers also to the abundance of oysters served with wine and ale in the taverns of medieval Dublin.

To clinch the argument that, however busy foreigners may have been fishing off our shores in the Middle Ages, our own people were not so stupid as to neglect the wealth so much coveted by others, one may well ask why, if the people of Galway had no interest in sea-fishing, did the city have an active guild of sea fishermen? This guild is well documented. And why do we find in a document of 1498 about the Corpus Christi pageant in Dublin that there were mariners, salmon-takers and fishers' guilds involved, if Dublin really had no active seafaring community? For the 1498 pageant the two first named guilds were to provide 'Noah with his Ship' appropriately equipped and the fishers 'The Twelve Apostles'.

3

Ireland's Sea Fisheries at the Time of the Tudor Conquest

There seems every reason to suppose that Irish sea fisheries were reaching an unprecedented level of prosperity when the sixteenth-century Tudor conquest altered the whole trend of Irish economic development, reducing our island, which had slowly been emerging towards nationhood, to the status of a colony. While there were many other motives — strategic, political and economic — which motivated Tudor England to undertake its haphazard and piecemeal conquest, there is no doubt that the wealth of our sea fisheries was a powerful stimulus to the greed of the swashbuckling adventurers who played an important part in the conquest.

The most celebrated exposition by an English adventurer of the profit obtainable by seizure of the Irish fisheries (in which Spanish and Portuguese fishermen were declared to be far too deeply involved for England's comfort), is to be found in the *Discourse of Ireland* of 1572 by Sir Humphrey Gilbert, half-brother of the explorer and historian, Raleigh, and planner of the Munster Plantation. But as early as April 1543 Sir Anthony St Leger, Henry VIII's lord deputy, had been writing to his king describing Spanish participation in the fisheries off our southern coast and urging him to take them over for his country's benefit.

Many fifteenth-century Englishmen had put in claims for licences to operate fisheries off the coasts of Ireland. In 1515 a proposed English law spoke of abundant Irish exports of hake, ling, herring and other fish to France and England, and suggested an export levy. What part were people of our own country playing in exploiting the fisheries?

The people of Ireland at the start of the sixteenth century were emerging falteringly, later than the Portuguese, Spanish, French and English but earlier than the Germans or Italians, into true nationhood. A combination of English invasion and Irish petty, local provincialism, however, brought the process to a halt for another three centuries. But the process had been a genuine one, a function of the development within a static society of a number of vigorous, outward-looking communities — municipal, religious, and sometimes essentially rural — which were groping, like the people of the rest of Europe, towards a new age, the 'renaissance'. The Ireland of 1500 has left us imperishable treasures in stone of flamboyant Irish Gothic religious architecture and the typically Irish tower houses of contemporary lay lords. It was the Ireland whose merchant ships were well known in most of the major European ports from

Seville to Gdansk, carrying the exports which met most of the cost of the early sixteenth-century building boom. All authorities agree that our most important early sixteenth-century export was fish, and among the most vigorous of the forward-looking communities in Ireland at the time were those which caught fish.

The Galway fishermen's guild whose activities in the fifteenth century have been noted was still operating at least as late as 1619, so its members can safely be assumed to have been catching fish throughout the sixteenth century. We learn from the Carew Manuscripts that in 1560 'O'Donnell exchangeth fish always with foreign merchants for wine'. If that fish had first to be bought from foreign fishermen there would not have been much to say for the quality or quantity of the wine. In the much more likely event that the fish was caught by native Donegal fishermen it would seem that there was an active fishing community even in one of the most isolated areas of the basically rural Ireland of that age.

Burke mentions in his *Industrial History of Ireland* the export of hake from Duncannon and Waterford to France as late as 1590. Trocmé and Delafosse in their exhaustive survey, *Le Commerce Rochelais de la fin du XVe siècle et au début du XVIIe*, refer to the regular arrival at La Rochelle, in ships of their town of origin, of merchants from Galway, Cork, Kinsale, Waterford, Arklow, Dublin, Drogheda and Dundalk. The authors emphasise the importance both of the export of salt and the import of herrings in the commercial exchanges between these merchants from Ireland and La Rochelle. This points to the existence of a flourishing fishing industry in Irish hands along a large stretch of our coast.

Professor Bernard's monumental three-volume history, *Navires et Gens de Mer à Bordeaux: vers 1400 — vers 1550*, provides abundant evidence of the importation to Bordeaux of fish procured from Irish merchants. As early as 1497 we find one J. Mahon of Youghal

Facsimile from the Carew Manuscripts of the well-known tribute to the wealth of the fisheries controlled in the sixteenth century by the O'Donnells around the coast of Donegal.

importing wine in the *Marie-Jehan*, to be paid for by a return cargo partly of hake. In 1502 Morice Donylh (? Donnell), also of Youghal, imported wine for Kinsale, Waterford and Baltimore, much of which was to be paid for with herrings, hake and other fish. Later in the same year Rob. Thobyn, also of Youghal, brought to the same ports more wine, again in exchange partly for herrings and hake. In 1503 Richard Donnel of Youghal was importing wine to his native town and other Irish ports, again in exchange for hake and herring as well as hard cash, leather and an Irish cloak. In 1507 Rich. Naych of Kinsale is to be found loading hake there for Saint Michel. In 1517 David Terre of Cork was importing wine and loading fish in part exchange. In 1520 an interesting consortium of merchants of Youghal, Bordeaux and Florence shipped a large quantity of wine in a Breton ship to Youghal, once again to be paid for partly in hake.

Matherson's *Wales and the Sea Fisheries*, published by the National Museum of Wales, refers to the importation of Wexford-caught herrings in the 1560s to Milford and Carmarthen in Wexford ships and to the importation later in the same century of Irish codfish, herring, white fish and salmon to Beaumaris, 'sometimes in Welsh and sometimes in Irish vessels'. The Chester records also provide much information about the shipping to that port by Irishmen of Irish-caught fish in the sixteenth century. Nearly eighty tons of Irish herring were landed in 1582–3 and over ninety in both 1584–5 and 1587. In January 1566 Patrick Forlong of Wexford unloaded herring at Chester and on 25 February, 1566 William Weddington, master of the *George* of Wexford, landed from his ship eighteen barrels of white herring and 10,000 red herring. On 8 March the *John* of Wex-

ford, master Torner, brought in 10,000 red herring and thirty barrels of white herring. On 13 August 1526 the *Michael* of Dublin, master Birsall, had landed 360 'dry fish', and two days later Walter Fyan imported '2 doz. fish' in the *Francis* of Dublin. These are only some examples.

In the Society for Nautical Research's very authoritative *Mariner's Mirror*, Vol. 46 No. 2 of May 1960, the late Captain Anthony MacDermott wrote: 'It should be noted that there was far more seafaring on the south and west coasts of Ireland during the sixteenth century than later. O'Malley in Mayo,[*] O'Donnell in Donegal (known as the King of Fish from the extent of his trade), O'Sullivan Beare in Cork and Kerry, and other territorial chieftains all owned large fishing fleets and exported great quantities of salt herrings.' He refers to a large trade in salt fish from Connacht to Spain and England, and recalls that O'Sullivan Beare granted a fishing licence to Spaniards which he refused to English applicants.

Froude, in Volume X of his *History of England*, mentions a report delivered in 1567 to Philip II of Spain which states that Waterford was a regular exporter of fish to Galicia, Portugal, Andalusia and Biscay. These fish would surely have been Irish-caught. They were exported in Irish ships.

An interesting reference is given in Richard Pearse's *The Ports and Harbours of Cornwall* to St Ives's sixteenth-century trade with Ireland, and in particular to the St Ives fishing nets: 'these were said to have been braided in the Dungarvan mesh'. This Irish town was described by Robert Cogan, Inspector of Customs, in 1611 as 'a poor fisher-

---

[*] The 14th. century Gaelic poet O'Dugan wrote that "a good man there never was of the Uí Máille but a mariner", as he was translated.

A rigged model of a sixteenth century herring buss, c. 1584

town' of which the chief trade was fish 'taken there', which was 'hake in great abundance, herrings and salmon', amounting to an annual export of £1,000, no small sum when it is remembered that Dungarvan was little more than a large village then, and beer was being sold at little more than 2d. a gallon.

A.K. Longfield says, in *Anglo-Irish Trade in the Sixteenth Century*, that 'fish was undoubtedly the most important product of sixteenth-century Ireland'. At the end of the century there was a tax of one night's fishing on every boat fishing from our coast every season, which it would not have been worth proposing unless there had been plenty of such boats. Earlier, there had been complaints that so much Irish-caught fish was exported that little or none was available for the home market. That this has a modern ring is perhaps evidence that the industry today has at last achieved a condition of prosperity comparable with what it enjoyed in the sixteenth century.

Longfield mentions that the customs records for the inland English port of Gloucester in the sixteenth century are very fragmentary. Yet the one week completely recorded shows a local ship importing herrings from Waterford, some caught by the ship herself, on which no duty had to be paid, but some on which duty was paid, implying that it was Irish-caught. Longfield also has references to Irish-caught haddock from Ross and cod from Wexford being landed at Bristol in 1588 and 1591, references to Kinsale's reputation for fishing pilchard, herring and hake, and comments on the popularity in England of oysters and probably clams from Ireland. She quotes a Bristol lawsuit of 1543 in which it noted that 'men of Erland' (Ireland) resorted to Bristol with *their* fish, which the local citizens bought for retailing in

the surrounding countryside.

Longfield shows that in 1504—5 121 ships imported fish to Bristol from Ireland, eighty-two of them English and the other thirty-nine from Irish ports — Waterford (13), Kinsale (7), Cork (6), Ross (4), Wexford (3), Youghal (2) and four others. The total value of the fish landed from Ireland was £2,465 4s. 8d. and the Irish ships provided more than 40 per cent of the value of landed fish, more than 66 per cent of this in the Waterford vessels. Bridgewater, much smaller than Bristol, was visited in 1560—1 by forty-five Irish ships importing fish — herrings, salt fish, clams, and porpoise — thirty-five of them from Wexford, the others from Youghal, Dungarvan, Cork and Waterford. This means nearly one Irish ship per week, many more than ever make their way up the swift-flowing Parret today, though this author did make the trip twenty-five years ago in an Arklow coaster with a cargo of powdered milk.

Even more convincing with regard to the existence of a genuine native fishing industry in the sixteenth century is Longfield's mention of Christ Church cathedral's legal worries in 1577 about enforcing its right to tithe on herrings caught. She gives the names of three fishermen involved, Thomas Heiwarde of Malahide, Thomas Carre of Howth and Patrick Managhan of 'Clontarfe'.

A hint of the importance and size of the fishing community in the Waterford area is to be found in the wording of a charter granted in March 1593 to the Mayor and Commons of Waterford. It refers to the 'blockhouse' built at the ferry within the city 'for the maintenance of good rule and order among the fishermen', and authorises the mayor, sheriff and citizens to impound herrings and other fish from the local fishermen to help pay for fortifications (this was in the period when the authorities in Ireland feared a Spanish invasion).

In 1588–9 156 vessels, 33 of them Irish, brought cargoes from Ireland to Chester and Liverpool, from Dublin, Drogheda, Carlingford and Dundalk, Waterford, Wexford and Ross, Dungarvan, Ardglass and Carrickfergus. They brought herring, salmon, cod, whiting and haddock, once more in proportionately larger quantities than the more numerous English ships.

Perhaps the most remarkable testimony to the numbers and expertise of the Irishmen engaged in the sixteenth-century fishing industry is to be found in the records of importation into England in Irish ships of cod caught apparently by Irishmen off the Newfoundland Banks. The first Europeans to see Newfoundland since the Vikings were probably the Italian Cabots sailing for Henry VII of England in 1497. Adventurous Portuguese and French navigators soon followed and, by the 1530s, the French were exploiting the Newfoundland cod fisheries in a big way. One of the consequences was a passion for eating cod, plentiful now for the first time, at the court of Francis I of France. Bristol Channel fishermen also began to fish in large numbers off Newfoundland, and Irishmen were at least as quick to take advantage of this development. This meant crossing the stormy North Atlantic there and back, a voyage of more than 4,000 miles, less than fifty years after Columbus dumbfounded Europe by proving that to cross and recross that ocean was not the impossibility everyone supposed. Yet the fishermen of Ireland apparently faced the hazard with the skill and courage, in vessels of fifty tons and much less, as the saintly scholars of a thousand years before.

As early as 1537 the *Mighell* of Kinsale, master Colman, reached Bristol with John Roche on board importing '4,000 of salt fish of the New Land, value £30', and Edmund Mollege with 1,000. At Padstow in 1557 another Kinsale ship landed '400 pisci terre nove (Newfoundland fish) de la smalle sorte'. In 1585 John Birmyngham in the *Sondaie* of Dublin landed 'one thousand and half of Newfoundland fishe, val. £20' at Chester. The *George* of Wexford had landed 120 small Newfoundland fish there in 1566. In due time, of course, Newfoundland, and also the adjacent French island of St Pierre, came to be peopled by large numbers of fishermen from Ireland, many of whose descendants with their identifiable Irish names remain seafarers to this day (the first St Pierrais to volunteer for the Free French Navy when St Pierre was liberated from the Vichyites in 1942 was the fisherman Walsh). There seems no reason to doubt that even if the *George, Sondaie* and so on had not themselves caught the Newfoundland fish they landed in England, it had been brought to Ireland by Irish fishermen.

By the end of the sixteenth century the old order in Ireland was about to pass away with the collapse of the great O'Neill's rebellion. By 1600, Longfield writes, 'Waterford and Wexford were the only towns which kept up the numbers of their craft, for in 1598 . . . they had more ships than all Ireland besides' and 'the prosperity of the fishing traffic declined' and 'the export of fish to England was naturally affected by the state of the country'. The author, however, attributes the falling off of our fishing industry as much to the competition of Newfoundland fish as to political reasons connected with the English conquest and she may be right. The sixteenth century, however, had unquestionably seen a prosperous

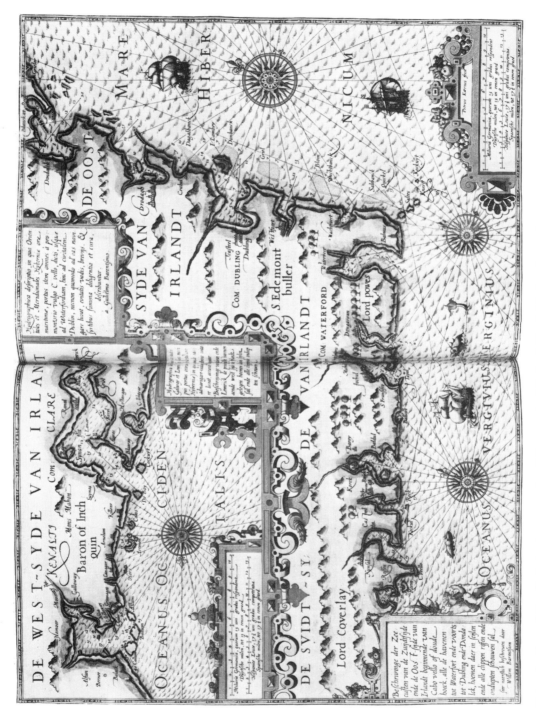

Reproduction of the first chart ever made of the coast of Ireland (Probably by the explorer Barendts) from the 1596-7 edition of Waghenaer's Nieuwen Spieghel der Zeevaart

Irish fishing industry.

The history of the industry refutes the myth that in medieval and Tudor Ireland any shipping and fishing carried on was in the hands of people of Anglo-Norman descent only. Whatever restrictions English governments and officials tried to impose, Gaelic-named Irish filtered steadily into the towns and became merchants, shipmasters and sea-fishermen alongside their fellow-citizens of other origins. Hence the Malachy Hogans, Richard Donnells, J. Mahons, Nicholas Duffs, William Kellys, John Goughs and so on that litter the pages of the Bristol, Bordeaux and Chester port records, testimony alike to the nascent if cruelly aborted nationhood of sixteenth-century Ireland, and to our ancestors' indomitable determination to face all perils of the green and greedy seas.

4

Ireland's Sea Fisheries from the Tudor Conquest to the Act of Union

The erratic course of our fishing industry between 1600 and 1800 was not the result of any sudden unwillingness on the part of Irishmen to face the seas on which their ancestors had thriven, nor of any alleged natural Irish antipathy to the sea. It was a consequence of the sudden interruption of the natural organic growth of the Irish economy and with it of course its fisheries, its most outstanding feature in the fifteenth and sixteenth centuries. In just the same way the irruption of Europeans into Asia and America in the sixteenth century shattered the natural development of those continents, providing 'proof' to the deliberately blind of the 'backwardness' of their peoples, or their land-lubberliness, in comparison with the sea-dogs of the Netherlands, England, France and the Iberian Peninsula.

Irishmen continued to fish the seas in the seventeenth and eighteenth centuries and more and more made names for themselves as seamen under foreign flags. But Irish fishermen were faced with innumerable problems arising directly out of the colonial condition in which the country was held at least until 1780. The most fundamental problem was the lack of a steady flow of capital into the industry. Such a flow there had obviously been in the preceding centuries, though we shall have to wait for a new generation of

historians aware of maritime matters to uncover the mechanism by which it worked. In the seventeenth and eighteenth centuries there were, from time to time, schemes, often quite generously financed, genuinely aimed to help our fishermen to help themselves; but more often they were conceived for the profit of foreigners or more or less rootless local entrepreneurs. Some schemes died because they were unrealistic, others because of a loss of interest. Few if any reflected the wishes of or were based on discussion with the fishermen themselves; all those years ago the fishing community proved that imposed solutions to its problems are both unacceptable and unworkable. Moreover, the years under review were years when more or less unconsciously industry and commerce were slowly beginning to adapt the findings of the slowly growing body of European scientists to their own ends. (One of the greatest gifts to humanity of the Renaissance was the idea that practical activities could profitably be guided by theory. Ineluctably, if gradually, the idea spread.) But in the fishing industry in Ireland before the days of Grattan's Parliament, the concept of an application of science to economic practice was virtually unknown.

Fishing in the centuries before the

Flight of the Earls in 1607 had grown up fragmentarily but organically in different parts of the country. It had become an economically and socially important factor in the life of many of the diverse communities of which Ireland was then composed. Now for the first time in its long history the Irish people were united under a single, strong government. Unfortunately it was an alien government, whose primary purpose was not the furtherance or protection of the Irish people's interests. Fishing in Ireland, as the result of Newfoundland competition, the growing strength of the fishing industry in the newly-independent Netherlands and in England itself, and other economic changes in Europe, required for the first time the sort of governmental encouragement which the Netherlands and English governments were giving; it required a unified policy, not the haphazard local growth which had hitherto sufficed. And precisely now, because the unification which had come about was imposed and was not the consequence of natural growth, no such policy was forthcoming.

The industry was still a force in 1611 if we are to believe Robert Cogan, Inspector of Customs. He listed the exports of various towns — Wexford, exporting herrings; Youghal, salmon; Kinsale which 'depends most upon fishing of pilchards, herring and hake'; and the 'poor fisher town' of Dungarvan, whose chief trade was 'transport of the fish taken there', hake in great abundance, herrings and salmon. He had not yet assessed towns further north but believed their trade consisted 'chiefly of fishing for salmon and herring, which is in great abundance'. Sir Oliver St John, in *A Description of the Province of Connacht* written in 1614, said of Galway that its 'merchants are rich and great adventurers at sea', and we know from a local

jury of 1609 the names of 'Connor Duffe, fisherman, Davy O'Ffodaghe, boatman' and 'Loughlin, fresh-water fisherman'. Ardglass was certainly still exporting fish early in the seventeenth century.

The Irish House of Commons adopted a bill in 1615 to restrain all foreigners from fishing off the Irish coast which certainly would have protected and encouraged local fishermen. James I's government in London, however, which could exercise a veto on decisions taken by the parliament in Dublin, refused to authorise the bill, and again in 1634 the parliament in Dublin passed a bill regulating the herring industry, but the new king, Charles I, refused his assent. Evidently there were, even in the not very representative Irish parliaments under the Stuart Kings, Irishmen who realised that the country needed an overall fisheries policy. Charles I's viceroy, Strafford, believed that fisheries could be developed in Blacksod Bay and claimed credit for an arrangement with the Spanish government for some kind of joint exploitation of these, but as early as 1627 the government in London was insisting on an extra tax on all pilchards, herrings and salmon exported from Ireland to lands other than England. With such restrictions and discouragements it is not surprising to read that Irish fishing declined while French, Spanish, Scottish and English fishermen throve from fishing in our waters, and the government of the Netherlands was allowed special fishery rights here in return for paying £30,000 to the ever-impecunious Charles I.

Nevertheless, Irishmen continued to go to sea both to fish and to trade (the English State Papers for Ireland record a 100-fold increase in the volume of Irish shipping between 1630 and 1640). For instance, in the Louvain Papers of the Irish Franciscans, the late

Father Brendan Jennings found a note that in October 1628 the Irish Franciscans at Louvain got permission to import two tons of salt fish landed by Irish sea captains, possibly fishermen. In 1641, just at the end of a period of thirty-eight years of comparative peace, and despite problems caused by an interruption of salt supplies from La Rochelle (in rebellion against the French king) and the activities of Algerian corsairs off our coasts, 41.5 tons of hake, salmon worth £7,300, pilchards worth £12,600 (12.63 tons — a bad year — £20,000 had been the recent annual value) and herrings worth £20,000 were exported. (The pound, of course, then still bought more than 100 times as much as today in terms of everyday commodities.)

This was a period when the energetic first Earl of Cork had been trying to develop the south Munster fisheries, building boats and establishing fish depots and salting centres. Irish pilchards were then considered the best in Europe, and were caught in quantities off the Cork coast. Dr A.E.J. Went, the Department of Fisheries' former well-known inspector, gave a fascinating paper on 'Pilchards in the South of Ireland' to the Cork Historical and Archaeological Society in 1946. He recalled that 'the State papers and other documents' afford strong evidence from about 1611 of the importance in parts of that century of the pilchard fishery. He cites the example of the Earl of Cork in 1616 paying £41 each to Oliver St John and a Mr Waynmothe and £20 to 'young Davies' to organise pilchard catching off Ardmore, exports of pilchards from Kinsale in 1617 and 1630, and the pilchard curing stations at Baltimore in 1631. The Earl of Cork also established a pilchard fishery at Crookhaven from which in 1627 pilchards were exported as far away as Marseille,

A Skerries Hooker, 20 to 50 tons, reproduced from The Deep Sea and Coast Fisheries of Ireland *by Wallop Brabazon, 1848*

but in a Dutch ship. Bantry, Dr. Went suggests, probably owes its very existence to the pilchard fishery and he provides proof of its flourishing state in 1622. Dr Went also thinks that it was for the pilchard fishery that the seine net was at this time introduced to Ireland. He gives an interesting description of seine net fishing:

In Ireland, the most important method of fishing the pilchard in the nineteenth and earlier centuries was the seine net. Two boats, the seine boat and the so-called 'follower', were used in the fishery. The seine boat, a large boat pulled by perhaps a dozen or more oars, carried the net, which was often up to 300—400 yards long. An experienced fisherman acted as 'huer' (hewer) by directing fishing operations from suitable points of vantage. From high land the huer could see the shoals of pilchards clearly and he directed the 'skipper' of the seine boat by suitable signs to the location of a likely shoal. On the given sign the net was shot around the shoal by the seine boat, every muscle of the oarsmen being exerted to speed the boat through the water and complete the circle. In the meantime the free end of the net was picked up by the 'follower' (a smaller boat, with a crew of perhaps five or six) and the two ends of the net were brought together. Stones or weighted pieces of timber, on ropes of suitable length, were splashed in the gap between the two ends of the net to prevent fish from escaping. The weighted foot-ropes of the net were gradually drawn up until the fish were completely enclosed in a purse of net. By means of baskets the fish were then gradually transferred from the net to the boat and fishing continued until no more fish could be managed, or if catches were poor, until darkness descended. Sometimes fishing was done by night when the fish were identified by the phosphorescence they caused in the water.

In 1628 'forty gentlemen' had applied for a patent 'with a view to overthrow the gain of the Hollanders by fishing, and to set twenty thousand people on work'. They set out the great potential of the Irish fishing industry as follows:

The Northern seas afford the Hollanders but two sorts of fish, cod and herrings. Ireland yields a great plenty of both, besides these several fishes following: pilchards, the best in Europe, which are vented in the Straits;* hake and cod much esteemed in Biscay; ray and conger for Britanny; salmon and buckthorn desired in all countries; cod and ling with the train oil that comes of them vented [sold] in England.

However, nothing came of their vision and even the Earl of Cork's and Strafford's efforts off the Munster and Mayo coasts led to only ephemeral developments. They were not rooted in the fishing communities themselves, and anyhow the wars of 1641—52 disrupted the whole economy of Ireland.

In 1672 the pioneer economist William Petty, usually reliable on economic facts, stated that there were only 1,000 people in the whole of Ireland engaged in fishing, of whom 'about twenty gentlemen who have engaged in the pilchard fishing, and have among them about 160 saynes [seines] wherewith they sometimes take about four thousand hogsheads of pilchards worth about ten thousand pounds.' He went on 'Cork, Kinsale and Bantry are the best places for eating of fresh fish,

* Straits of Dover.

(66)

It is Judged best to Land. There is no Castle or Fort
Except Carrickfergus upon this River

Old Fleet or Lough=Larn

Is a good but narrow Harbour to go in for Ships
of 200 or 300 Tuns, if acquainted. the Lough may hold
250 or 300 Ships. men of War may anchor and Ride
in the Bay without the Harbour. the Ships may Lye
a Ground or a float and can come very near the
Moar but the Ground is Soft and Muddy, and therefore
inconvenient to Land men or Horse without Boats.
the best Ground for Landing is about Cirrel Castle
Which is a place without any Fort the north Side
is best to Land
There are no other good Harbours
between Waterford and the Lough of Derry
This Examination I have taken
from Anthony Wild of Belfast
James Shearer of Donnayhadee } Masters of Ships
John Magee of Ballyshannon
William Mercer of Limerick

Confirmed by
William Howard of Chester } Masters of Ships
James Briscoe of Chester
Robert Nevil of Londⁿ

Presented to his Grace the Duke of
Schonberg Wednesday July 24. 1689. By A: B:
V: H:

Extract from a survey of Irish harbours, referring to Larne, and carried out by W. Molyneux in 1689

(Right and following pages) Facsimile of a letter written by Robert Southwell from Kinsale in 1671, drawing attention to the incursions of French fishing vessels into the herring, mackerel and pilchard fisheries off Co. Cork, and the injurious effects of these incursions on the local hooker fleet

I am also humbly bold to acquaint your Ex:^{cie} that here are come
upon this Coast thirty or forty of ffrench fishing vessells each burthen
thirty or forty Tunns haveing very long Strings, and Rafts of Netts
which they call Mackrell Netts, But they have both Mackrell
and herring Meath, the Mackrell netts they place uppermost
and next unto ye Roses, and the herring netts under, that in the
same Raft and both joynd together, each vessell haveing a
thousand netts, and about thirty or forty men carryes out in
length ab^t the distance of two miles all their men armed wth
musketts and firelocks as is said.

By means of these long and unlawfull netts they
utterly breake and destroy the great Skulls of ffish of what kind
soever comeing upon this coast to ye great destruction of that
trade of fishing by his Ma^{ts} Subjects in these parts, and in
perticulor the undertakers of the Pilchard fishing in the
west of Ireland provided and set forth at very vast and great
charges of such undertakers, As also the hookers and
ffishermen of this Towne consisting of about sixty or
eighty boates and others of ye hookers and ffishermen of Youghall
Dungarvan, and all other the westerne parts of Ireland
to ye very great disheartening and impoverishing of
them, and also the abatem^t and Lessening of that
branch of his Ma^{ts} Revenue of the Customes & excise
arriseing upon that trade, and employm^t of the ffishers by
his Ma^{ts} Subjects on this coast, who pay his Ma^{ts} duties
upon ye salt and other provisions inwards, and also his Ma^{ts}
duties of Custome and excise both on fish and trayne outwards
whereas these Strangers and fforraines that fish on the
Coast pay neither

Before these ffrench vessells used the Coast it was very
usuall wth ye hookers and ffishermen of Kinsale only wth 3 men &

sometimes a boy in each boat to take three or fower thousand
Mackrell in a day to a boat, wch were often salted into vessells
and sent into forraigne parts whereas now they take very few
or none at all and altogether fish growing very scarce by means
of these mens breaking the Skulls of fish.

200

My Lord, I have made bold to give you this acc^t vpon the Compl^ts
of the hookers fishermen, and others of this towne, and have also
thereinclosed made bold to send your Lo^pp a true Coppie of an order
of the right hono^ble the Lord Lieut and Councell dated the 15 of
June 1663. then sent vnto the Soveraigne of Kinsale, wch did
in good measure provide for the removall of this inconveniency
both to his Matie and his Subjects in these westerne parts. But
in regard there has not been of late yeares any of his Maties ships
or frigotts appointed to ye guard of this coast, wch might have
compelld obedience from these strangers vnto those his Maties and y^e
Councells orders they have not enjoyed the benefitt thereof and
they further complayne that ye times lymitted by the said order
to begin and end ye Mackrell fishing is not according to their
Rules and observation of those fishing Seasons, wch they say should
begin from ye first of Aprill in each yeare and to continue
to ye last o^f October following, And since there are not now
any of his Matie Ships vpon ye Coast to put ye said order in
execution, or to require obedience therevnto from those french
fishermen now fishing vpon this Coast, and that within lesse
then one league of the Shoare in severall parts. If your
Ex^cie and Councell may be pleased to renew ye said order with
Amendm^t and change of ye time for beginning the said Mackrell
fishing, And if it may stand wth your Lord^pps grave wisdomes to
Authorise & impower the hookers and fishermen of this towne
or any of them to cutt or seize their netts whereever they meet
wth them in y^e sea, & to bring them to shoare, and there to be tryed

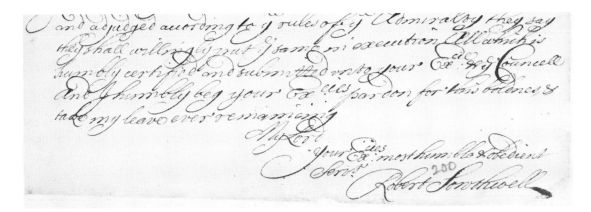

though Dublin be not or need not be ill-supplied with the same.' Dean Swift's first employer, Sir William Temple, said 'the fish of Ireland might prove a mine under water as much as any underground'. But he complained of the absence of the necessary manpower and of the cheapness of other foods militating against the growth of a home-market.

Petty established pilchard fisheries in Kenmare Bay and at Dursey Island, and Viceroy Ormonde took what steps the administration in London allowed to try to revive the Irish fisheries. In 1672 luggers captured from the Dutch, Europe's leading fishermen, during an Anglo-Dutch war, were sent to Ireland to help. The efforts of Ormonde, Petty and others were hampered on the one hand because they were, once again, imposed rather than developed in co-operation with the surviving fishing communities, and on the other hand because vast fishing fleets were off our coasts and treating our fisheries as their own. These fleets came from France, now Europe's richest state and of which the later Stuart kings of England were virtual puppets. A letter from Kinsale quoted in the State Papers for 1671 describes large French fishing vessels with up to forty men aboard all armed with firearms causing havoc to the mackerel, herring and pilchard fisheries of the south and west.

Nevertheless, the same letter declares that till recently there were sixty to eighty fishing boats operating out of Kinsale, each carrying three men and a boy and catching 3 to 4,000 mackerel daily. The same letter, incidentally, contains a very early reference to the famous Kinsale hooker, a fishing craft which survived into the early years of this century, the construction and operation of which is yet one more tribute to the ingenuity of the Irish fisherman. The Kinsale hooker, developed for line fishing, was a local adaptation of a Dutch fishing boat design.

The British Survey of Fishing Boats and Coastal Craft round these islands published by His Majesty's Stationery Office for the Science Museum in 1950 contains an interesting section on Ireland. It includes references to the very sophisticated currachs and illustrations of them — one sailing and one under construction — drawn by Captain T. Phillips in about 1685 and now in the Pepysian Library, Cambridge. These vessels were much more advanced in design than the currach of today. It mentions also sketches of Irish fishing boats of about 1700, showing the rig of that period as two spritsails with mainmast stepped amidships. Most con-

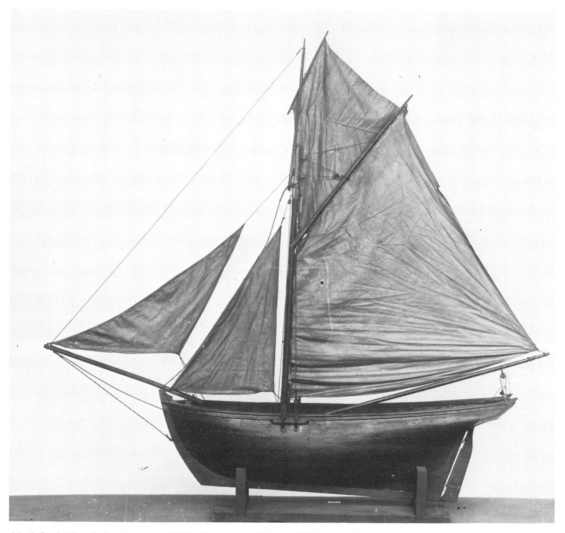

Model of Kinsale hooker, a middle distance offshore fishing craft with gaff cutter

temporary Irish fishing craft were double-ended, and the Survey's author, E.W. White, AMINA, notes that 'Skerries yawls from the neighbourhood of Bally-castle, Co. Antrim, still retain both the pointed stern and this double spritsail rig'.

In 1665 Ireland exported 16,252 barrels of herring (compared with 23,311 in 1641) and this fell to 12,893 in 1669; salmon exports were 526 tons in 1641, 330 in 1665 but in 1669 went up to 905; pilchard exports were

1,263 tons in 1641, 332 in 1665 but went up to 795 in 1669; hake exports were negligible in 1665, slightly improved in 1669 but still fewer than in 1641; train oil exports, also negligible in 1665, surpassed the 96 tons of 1641 by 11 tons in 1669. In spite of all problems, by 1689 the fishermen of Ireland, apparently increasing again in numbers, were once more exporting in a big way. George O'Brien discovered a document that recorded that in that year 'the cargoes of salmon, herrings and pil-

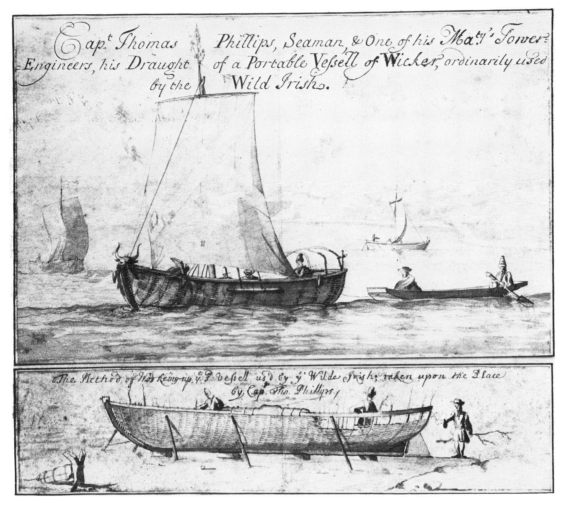

A sailing currach and a sailing currach under construction, c. 1685. Drawn by Captain T. Phillips

chards and other fish made up yearly in Ireland and transported into several ports of Spain and Venice and of the ports in the Mediterranean Sea would startle common people'.

References to large exports of ambergris to England and Spain, especially by Galway merchants, in the seventeenth century suggest that whale-catching was also practised by Irishmen at that time. According to Petty in his *Political Anatomy*, moreover, 'they [the Irish] can everywhere gather cockles, oysters, muscles [sic], crabs, etc. with boats, nets, angles, or the Art of Fishing'. In 1698 complaints were made in ports of England near the Straits of Dover about 'the Irish catching herrings at Waterford and Wexford, and sending them to the Straits', thereby ruining their markets; and there were even suggestions put up to the English government that only English fishermen should be let fish in Irish waters. But all this is proof that notwithstanding all kinds of obstacles (including exclusion of Irishmen in Charles II's reign from the Newfoundland fisheries), Irish fishermen

"A currach from the Boyne" (model) in use c. 1700. Reproduced from British Fishing and Coastal Craft *by E. W. White*

were still successfully plying their trade round our coasts.

King William III, one of Irish history's legendary demons, sent instructions that the native Irish fishing industry must be encouraged, but his successor Queen Anne, like the rest of the Stuarts, permitted steps to be taken in the opposite direction. An act of the English parliament (2 and 3 Anne c. 16) put obstacles in the way of the importation here of rock salt, essential for fish curing.

This Act of Anne's reign introduces the story of the Irish fisheries in the eighteenth century, which ran a course as erratic as it had in the century before. 'For the first half of the eighteenth century', wrote Burke in his *Industrial History of Ireland,* 'the Irish fisheries did not attract the attention of the home or of the English government.' The Newfoundland fisheries having been reopened to Irishmen in 1704, it seems that the most enterprising of our fishermen were tempted to emigrate and engage in the lucrative fisheries of the transatlantic island. By 1793, it is believed, the majority of the residents of Newfoundland were Irish and fishing was by far the most important of the local industries.

By 1729 we seem to have been importing more fish than we exported, perhaps for the first time, and there were complaints of the fishermen's 'unskilfulness and want of enterprise'.

This complaint was despairingly re-echoed in the presence of this author some 230 years later by the late President Childers when he was Parliamentary Secretary in charge of fisheries and accused Irish fishermen at a Dun Laoghaire Chamber of Commerce dinner of being 'bloody-minded'. The fact was that in the 1720s as in the 1950s there was an immense gulf of suspicion and misunderstanding, literally centuries old, between government and fishermen, and it has taken a series of developments of fundamental importance — the creation of An Bord Iascaigh Mhara, the foundation of fishermen's organisations, the start of trade union interest in the lot of deck-hands in fishing craft, a drive for the proper training of sea-fishermen, and a sustained interest on the part of enlightened sections of the public — to revive a sense of reasoned optimism about the future of our sea fishing industry.

In 1739 there was a complaint that many fishing towns in Ireland were in great poverty because of disgraceful neglect of the fisheries; in 1755 it was pointed out that there was not a single large fishing vessel in the whole island and no well-capitalised company as in England to promote sea fishing, and in

A Connemara hooker.(Compare this with the Kinsale hooker on p. 36)

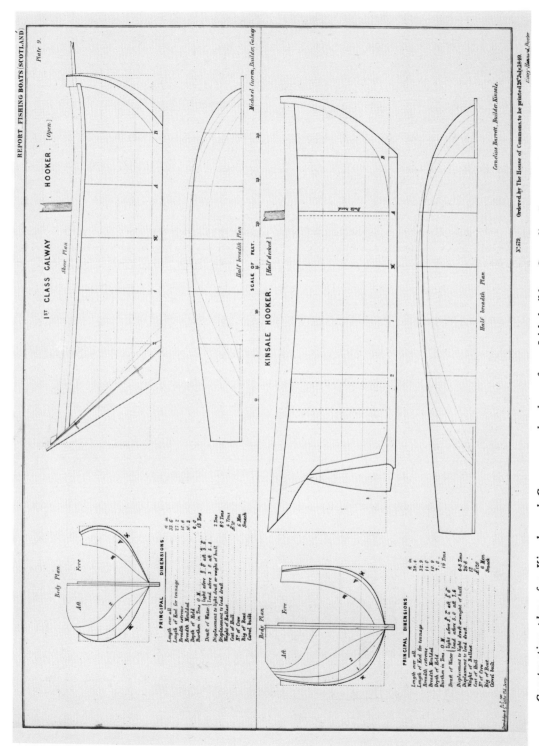

Construction plans for Kinsale and Connemara hookers, from Irish builders Cornelius Barrett of Kinsale and Michael Curran of Galway, 1849

CHAPTER XVI. (¹)

AN ACT for the better securing and regulating the Duties upon Salt

WHEREAS great Sums of Money are paid out of Her Majesties Duty upon Salt on Account of Debentures for Salt shipped to be exported to Forreigne Parts and it is found by Experience that great Part of the Salt for which such Debentures have been paid hath been fraudulently landed on the Coasts of England and Wales and not exported to any Forreign Parts or haveing been actually landed in Ireland or other Places out of England and Wales have been shipped off againe from thence and fraudulently brought into England or Wales by which evill Practices Her Majesties said Dutyes are very much lessened in the Produce thereof and the Salt-makers who pay their full Dutyes are very much prejudiced and discouraged in their Trade by reason they cannot sell their Salt in Places which are supplied with Salt run as aforesaid For Remedy whereof Be it enacted by the Queens most Excellent Majestie by and with the Advice and Consent of the [Llords'] Spirituall and Temporall and Commons in this present Parliament assembled and by Authority of the same That no Salt whatsoever being of the Produce or Manufacture of England Wales Berwick upon Tweed Scotland or Ireland nor any other Salt coming from Ireland Scotland or the Isle of Man shall after the First Day of June One thousand seven hundred and four be imported or brought into any Port or Place within England Wales or Berwick upon Tweed nor be taken out of any Shipp or Vessell nor put on Shore within any of the said Ports or Places upon Pain that all the Salt so imported or brought in taken out of any Shipp or Vessell or landed or put on Shore contrary to the true Intent and Meaning of this Act shall be forfeited and lost and that the Shipp or Vessell in which any such Salt shall be so imported or brought in or out of which any such Salt shall be taken or put on Shore together with all her Tackle and Apparell shall also be forfeited and lost and every Person that shall take any such Salt out of any such Shipp or Vessell or carry the same on Shore or convey the same from the Shore when landed or be aiding or assisting therein shall forfeit the Sum of Twenty Pounds for every such Offence or suffer Six Months Imprisonment

Extract from Act of 1700 for better securing and regulating the duties upon salt (2 and 3 Anne, c. 16)

1772 Irish fishermen were accused of being half their time idle and greatly prone to drunkenness. These references were garnered by George O'Brien for his *Economic History of Ireland in the Eighteenth Century*. The historian Lecky attributed the industry's decline in part to the introduction about 1738 of the 'trailing net' (trawl) and in part to the desertion of the coast by fish shoals. These may well have been factors, but the real cause of the trouble was more deeply seated.

Bantry was still exporting pilchards and Dungarvan hake and haddock in the first half of the century. Later their trade collapsed, though as late as 1758 Dr Pococke, Church of Ireland Bishop of Ossory, wrote of Sherkin Island:

They are all fishermen both in this island and Cape Clear; & they have on the coast, places for curing fish, commonly call'd fish palaces, & [fishermen ?] come to these parts from Cork and Kingsale, most especially about Crookhaven which abounds in fish, & make little huts in which they live during the Summer; most in time of peace the French come over here to fish: where the pilchards came great fortunes were made by them: Now they get chiefly Mackrel during the months of July & August.

And the natural aptitude of Irish fishermen for their trade was shown in 1754 when some were brought to the Scottish island of Uist to teach the locals the secret of turning seaweed to kelp, launching thus a flourishing industry.

Changes for the better gradually occurred. As early as 1738 the Irish parliament granted bounties on fins and oil for the encouragement of whaling and in 1763 £1,000 was voted to stimulate the industry off Donegal. But the capital advanced was insufficient and the official interest shown too irregular and remote, so that by the end of the century the once promising Irish whale fishery was dead. (It was revived for a while by Norwegians at Inishkea and Blacksod early in this century. Dr. J.S. Fairlie of UCG has recently written a book on the history of the Irish whale fisheries entitled *Irish Whales and Whaling*, published by the Blackstaff Press).

In 1763 more valuable stimulants were provided by parliament in the form of subsidies on fish exports and for every fishing vessel over 20 tons in operation. And in 1766, foreshadowing important aid to the fisheries in decades to come, the recently founded Royal Dublin Society offered premiums for the setting up of coast fisheries.

As ever, Irish fishermen responded when some effort was made to meet their interests. Herring exports rose again and by 1773 exports out of Cork alone were valued at £21,000 annually. Arthur Young, who began his 'Tour in Ireland' in 1776, wrote of 400 boats fishing for herring off the Ards Peninsula, 500 in Lough Swilly and 327 off Killybegs, and of 10,000 herrings per boat as the average catch in Killala's October herring season of two to three weeks. Young also described the flourishing fishermen's co-operatives, the men dividing the profits so that each was worth from ten to sixteen shillings a

A model of a two-masked Wexford cot with centre plate. Built during the mid eighteenth century these boats were fully planked, flat-bottomed and had a double gaff schooner rig similar to those of the eighteenth and early nineteenth century Irish wherries. This rig was identified with the Irish east coast and perpetuated into the twentieth century in the case of the Swansea pilot boats

XXII. And be it enacted by the authority aforefaid, That from and after the twenty fourth day of June one thoufand feven hundred and fixty all boats, except gabbards and ferry-boats, belonging to any port or place, or plying at any port or place from the port of Wexford inclufive to Rufh, and fo northward to the port of Londonderry inclufive, fhall be regiftered by the refpective owners of fuch boats in the offices of the cuftomers, or collectors of fome one of the diftricts within that coaft; which officers are hereby required to keep proper books for that purpofe, and to regifter fuch boats upon demand by the owner or owners thereof; who fhall give a notice in writing to fuch officer, expreffing the name and burthen of fuch boat, and alfo the name or names of the owner or owners thereof, and of his or their place of abode; all which particulars fuch regifter fhall contain : and every mafter, owner, or other perfon navigating the faid boat, fhall on or before every intended voyage to the faid ifle of Man take out a permit for fuch voyage under the hand of fome one of the officers of the revenue employed upon the coaft, or ftationed in or near the port or place, to which fuch boat fhall belong; and fhall likewife mention to the officer the name and names of every mariner to be employed in navigating fuch boat to the faid ifland, in order that the faid names may be inferted in fuch permit; and alfo on his return from the faid ifland deliver up fuch permit to be cancelled to the collector, or other officer of the port or diftrict, where he fhall arrive; or, in cafe the fame fhall be loft, make oath before fuch officer (who is hereby impowered to adminifter the fame) of the lofs thereof, on pain of forfeiting the fum of twenty pounds: provided always, that in fuch permit it fhall (if defired by the mafter or owner of fuch boat) be inferted, that he goes out in order to fifh for herrings; and that the mafter or owner of any boat, having fuch permit, fhall not be obliged to return fuch permit during the feafon of the herring-fifhery, which is from the firft day of July to the firft day of November; which permit fuch officer is hereby required on demand to grant without fee or reward upon pain of forfeiting to fuch perfon, as fhall be refufed fuch permit, or be unneceffarily delayed in obtaining the fame, the fum of ten pounds, to be recovered by civil bill or action of debt.

All boats (except gabbards and ferry-boats) from Wexford northward to Derry, fhall be regiftered by the officer on demand by owner, and notice in writing of the name, burthen, owner's name and abode.

Mafter thereof, &c. before intended voyage to ifle of *Man* fhall take permit from an officer, in which everymariner's name inferted, on return, delivered to the officer where he arrives, to be cancelled, or oath made of the lofs, penalty 20l. inferted in permit (if defired) that the mafter goes out for herrings, not obliged to return it from 1 July to 1 November. Permit granted on demand, without fee,on pain of 10l. to party refufed or delayed.

Extract from an Act of 1763 introducing the compulsory registration of boats and the introduction of a herring season confined to July 1st until November 1st (33 Geo. II, c.10) week — a very reasonable income in those days, particularly when you think that farm workers in many parts of Ireland were earning less than double that number of shillings as late as the 1930s; and by then the shilling was badly devalued.

The ability of the best Irish fishermen to surmount all the problems nagging them in the eighteenth century can be further shown by an examination of the records of the chief ports of France. As far back as 1705 we find refugee merchants in Nantes named O'Riordan and Harper importing salt fish and herrings caught by Irish fishermen. In 1737 seventy-five ships reached that port from Ireland, thirty-eight of

them with cargoes for merchants of Irish birth or descent, many of the cargoes including fish. In 1736 an Irish ship discharged a cargo of Irish salted fish in far-off Marseille and on 27 February 1752 a brigantine of Cork captained by one Evan Hill discharged a cargo of Irish salmon there as well. One could go on.

When the events of 1780 and 1782 lifted first the legal restraints on Irish trade and then the constitutional restraints on the Irish parliament, the latter, corrupt though many of its members were and limited though its power still was owing to the fact that the London-appointed Irish government was not answerable to it, did take steps

Sea fish nets and lines cured with tar and oil, X. And whereas there is a very pernicious practice all round the west and north west coasts of Ireland of tanning or barking of nets, which practice is not only of little effect in regard to the first intention of preserving said nets, but on the contrary of infinite detriment to the growth of young trees, and destruction of plantations, through the villainous practice of stripping trees merely for the bark thereof in order to tan or bark nets for the herring, salmon, and other fisheries, notwithstanding there is a much more efficacious method of curing of nets less expensive, and in no shape detrimental to plantations, by curing said nets with tar and oil, which nets so cured may lie for a month wet without getting **not barked or tanned,** damage, whereas bark cured nets must be dried daily, or they will rot : be it therefore enacted by the authority aforesaid, That all nets for taking herrings, salmon, or any sea fish, and all fishing **or forfeited to informer.** lines cured after the passing of this act, shall be cured with tar and oil, and not barked or tanned, under penalty of the forfeiture of all such nets to the informer upon conviction before a justice of the peace.

Proof on owner of being made before. XI. And be it further enacted by the authority aforesaid, That all nets found tanned, and not tar and oil cured, the proof shall lie on the owner of said nets, that they were made prior to the passing of this act, or that they are nets that were made and cured before brought to the aforesaid west or north west coast ; in failure of such proof all such nets to be forfeited as aforesaid.

Extract from an Act of George III ordering the practice of tanning and barking of fishing nets to be discontinued in order to preserve young trees and plantations, and that the nets should be cured using tar and oil instead (1777)

An early print of Bullock Harbour, Co. Dublin by J. T. Serres, 1788. This had already been a fishing harbour for centuries

to encourage sea fishing. The duty on imported salt was very sharply reduced and subsidies were increased both for fish exports and for each fishing vessel over 20 tons operating; personnel grants were introduced to ensure a plentiful supply of naval recruits; and a scheme was organised, much in advance of its time both in conception and operation, for thorough inspections of the quality of all fish exported. Between 1779 and 1783 the annual herring export was 24,000 barrels, nearly five times what it had been fifteen years before, and in 1784 23,000 barrels were exported to the West Indies alone. In that year herrings sold at home at 10d. per 1000, yet millions are said to have been thrown away unsold: had many Irish people already by then lost the taste for fish, which was evidently lively in early and medieval times according to literature extant? Only now is the taste for fish slowly being revived, largely through the propaganda campaigns of An Bord Iascaigh Mhara.

It was said that small fishing vessels in 1784 made as much as £54 profit from a few months' herring fishing. In 1785, when the parliament raised the duty on imported herrings to protect the home industry, 35,514 barrels of herrings were exported, and in 1786, 1787 and 1790 more herrings were exported than imported. In 1788 and 1789 the average export was nearly 14,000 barrels and the average import 14,500. The herring exports to the West Indies brought in £7,200 in 1790, and there was a prosperous fishery in mackerel, cod and ling that year. Irish herrings had a fine reputation on the Continent and could command a price 14½ per cent above those caught by the British, whose herring merchants were accused of 'fraud, perjury, and all the tricks which ingenuity could invent to rob the public'. To put things more objectively as a British Commission of Enquiry into their fisheries did, the British had no inspection system like ours, no subsidy on salt used for curing as was introduced here in 1786, and too many 'unreasonable restraints' imposed on their fishermen.

During the last years of 'Grattan's Parliament' therefore, the Irish fishing industry was building up again at last. These were not only years when Dublin abounded in herrings and in 'cockles and mussels alive, alive-oh' (Molly Malone flourished at that period, I believe), but also years when Irish fishermen were specially invited to teach the art of fishing to the men of Shetland and Orkney, reckoned the finest seamen in these islands. They went further, for while the winter fishery from Burtonport alone was producing 'to the inhabitants of the Rosses a sum of £40,000' divided between nearly 300 vessels (McParlan's *Statistical Survey of Donegal*, 1802), other Irish fishermen were pouring into Newfoundland for the ever-lucrative cod-fishing there, and profiting from the recent English abolition of the ban on Irishmen in the whaling fleet, to flock into the flourishing Greenland whale fishery. Moreover, shipbuilding was also beginning to do well: as many as seventy-three ships were built in Ireland in 1790 and fifty in 1791, the year shipbuilding began in Belfast. In all, 515 ships totalling 23,550 tons were constructed in Ireland between 1788 and 1800, compared to only 346 totalling 18,362 tons in the succeeding decade.

If around 1790 it looked as though the Irish maritime economy was at last growing to the level of importance proper to an island-dwelling people, and if Grattan's Parliament was responsible for the process that established round Dublin Bay Europe's first organised lifeboat service (manned largely by fishermen), how do we account for the fact that by the time the Act of

XIV. And be it enacted by the authority aforefaid, That if any perfon or perfons fhall bring into any port, haven, or creek of this kingdom, any herrings which fhall not be good, fweet, feafonable, and meet for man's meat, or which fhall not be packed in barrels, or in bulk regularly and in layers, and not heaped together, unlefs the fame fhall be landed for the exprefs purpofe of fmoaking, where houfes are built exprefsly for that purpofe, in the manner of Yarmouth, commonly called red herrings, and fhall offer the fame to be fold, then all and every perfon or perfons, owners thereof, being convicted thereof before the chief magiftrate or collector of fuch port, haven, or creek, or any juftice of the peace, fhall lofe and forfeit the fame, and fuch part of faid fifh that is not good, fweet, and feafonable, fhall be thrown into the fea, and the reft fhall be forfeited for the ufe of the poor.

Perfons who bring herrings to any port, &c of this kingdom to be fold, which fhall not be meet for man's meat, and packed as herein, forfeit the fame. See 26 G. 3. c. 20. f. 4.

Extract from an Act passed by George III in 1785 stating that ill-packed herrings must be forfeited. This imposition of quality control was one of several steps taken by "Grattan's Parliament" between 1782 and 1800 to improve our sea fishing industry

Union was passed in 1800 that same maritime economy, despite a steadily rising population, was in a state of collapse? In 1800 only eighteen ships were built and herring exports at around £3,000 were less than one-seventh of the 1789—91 average.

The reasons are many. The 'free' parliament, though a more valuable instrument than its unfree predecessor, was dominated by greedy property-owners and corrupt place-seekers. When pressure was put upon the members by the government, to which the fisheries represented a very minor problem, the majority was ready to sell out every Irish interest for a bribe. There was consequently no consistent encouragement for the injection of capital into an industry which, even at its best, had attracted criticism for the smallness of its boats and the simplicity of the gear used.

Moreover, the 1790s were years of political unrest, leading first to war with France, which curtailed exports and exposed our fishermen to attack from ubiquitous French privateers, then to the 1798 rising. Incidentally, the Wexford United Irishmen made history by requisitioning a number of oyster-boats as a coast guard and reconnaissance flotilla, a notable episode in the story of Irish fishermen. Quite a lot of Irish seamen left the country to join the navy of revolutionary France, like the celebrated Murphy of Drogheda who eventually became chief pilot of the main French naval base at Brest. Others were pressed into or voluntarily joined the British navy.

There were further causes for the decline of the fisheries. Many of our most enterprising fishermen left for Newfoundland or whaling off Greenland. Foster's Corn Law and other boosts given by the 'free' parliament to agriculture led to a boom which enabled land to be subdivided and younger sons, who would otherwise have gone to sea, succumbed to the temptation to be landholders even if only on a minute scale. An almost total absence of the scientific knowledge, which we are now more and more seeing to be indispensable for a healthy fishing industry, meant that the unpredictable behaviour of the fish shoals, particularly erratic it seems in the 1790s, was another disheartening feature of the situation.

So Ireland entered the nineteenth century with her maritime economy and above all her fisheries, which ought to have been playing as vitalising and essential a part in the life of the country as in 1500 — and as we hope they will in 2000 — in a sad state of decay.

5

Ireland's Sea Fisheries from the Act of Union to the Famine

Innumerable questions have been asked and legends have arisen about the fishing industry and the Famine. Why were there so many deaths from disease directly attributable to starvation? people ask, if there were thousands of fishermen catching fish round our coasts as the official figures indicate. Answers vary from suggestions that the Irish fishermen of the time were either very bad fishermen, or very greedy and selfish, to the suggestion that the official figures were phoney. It is true, however, that the number of men and boys engaged in sea fishing went up from just over 21,000 in 1821 to just over 93,000 in 1845 and 113,000 in 1846. Few, however, have asked why the numbers went up and fewer still have seriously considered the actual situation of fishermen during the famine years.

The population rose rapidly between the Union and the Famine. There were limits to the number of people which the land, more and more subdivided, could support. Men were driven to fishing for a living. But the great majority lacked experience, virtually all lacked the capital necessary for success in highly competitive conditions, and they all lacked the backing of scientific research into the habits and habitats of fish shoals which developing scientific knowledge could even then have begun to provide.

The ramshackle and haphazard 'industry' which grew up in the second quarter of the century had scarcely a vestige of what is now called 'indispensable infrastructure'. Most of our ports were either dilapidated or in a rudimentary state. It was one of Thomas Davis's many sound economic demands in *The Nation* that our ports be developed ('put quays to our harbours', he wrote in his essay 'The Resources of Ireland') and a proper scheme of nautical instruction instituted. Railway construction was only in its infancy, roads were poor, the canals, already on the verge of decline, barely touched the areas most affected by famine. Retail shops were few and far between and, outside cities, no system of wholesale distribution had been set up.

How were our thousands of fishermen operating in tiny boats for the most part (the 113,000 fishermen of 1846 are credited with working no fewer than 19,883 boats), with primitive gear, inexperienced, and in sharp competition with each other, unorganised below, unguided from above, to systematise the distribution of what fish they caught to all those areas miles inland where famine was raging? Most of the 113,000 fishermen, however intelligent, would have had no education at all to fit them for dealing with such a complex problem. Furthermore, there is every reason to believe that in the mass of the population the taste for eating fish had ceased to exist; and experiences of United Nations agencies in our own day in famine-stricken areas show that it is very difficult to induce an unlettered populace suddenly to alter its diet even to save its life. The commissioners of Public Works reported in 1847 that country people would not eat fish without potatoes, which were of course unobtainable.

There seems no reason to suppose that many fishermen died of hunger, though thousands may have died of disease. Take the example of the family of John Philip Holland, the submarine pioneer, born at Liscannor, County Clare in 1841. His father was a coast guard and would inevitably have done some sea fishing. None of his family died of starvation but one son did die of cholera, the very infectious disease the diffusion of which was precipitated by the wide-spread hunger.

The 1840s were years when 'laissez-faire' ideas dominated economic thought. The fittest were supposed to survive by their own efforts in an environment of universal competition. It was the fate of the weaker to go to the wall. Those years were 'the hungry forties' all over Europe, even if hunger struck Ireland more devastatingly than other areas. Nowhere did governments believe in those days, or indeed till many decades later, that they had any obligation to organise or plan national economies. The idea of seeking the co-operation, still less the advice, of producers or working people would never have occurred to people in power in Europe in the 1840s. It is only tentatively and at that by no means everywhere applied today.

The untrained, under-capitalised Irish fishermen of the 1840s cannot be made to carry any responsibility for the Famine. But if the core of real, experienced fishermen of the early years of the century, or even of the 1840s themselves, had been consulted by any authority they might well have had proposals to make that could have mitigated the catastrophe that occurred, particularly if they had also had the support of an extra injection of capital investment into the industry and whatever fishery research knowledge was then obtainable. They might have been able to provide clues to the disappearance of the herrings reported to have occurred on the west coast at the height of the Famine. Was this a consequence of the operation in the 1840s, in the narrow limits in which such small vessels were able to fish, of too large a flotilla of fishing boats? Certainly, from the Union to the Famine, that hard core of sea fishermen which has carried on the tradition of sea fishing down the centuries was still able to make some contribution to the economy of our country.

Charles O'Brien's survey of Kerry in 1804 reveals that there were in the Dingle area 120 boats or hookers of from 10 to 15 tons, engaged in coastal trading in summer and fishing herring from September. Elsewhere in the county the boats were smaller and were hauled on to the beaches beneath the cliffs for safety in bad weather. In all, O'Brien estimated, Kerry had 798 boats fishing six months each year; with six hands per boat this meant 3,288 employed (O'Brien's arithmetic was curious — 6 x 798 = 4,788). There were more boats in the Kenmare river than anywhere else in the county, and only two harbours, Dingle and Valentia. Later O'Brien called Valentia 'perhaps one of the safest harbours in the world', which 'must become a great importance if ever the fishery on this

A fishing wherry at Dunleary pier, 1799. A print by F. Jukes

An early view of Kingstown Harbour. This was when Dun Laoghaire Harbour was under construction in the 1820s. It quickly became an important fishing port

coast meet encouragement'. He said wherries from Rush and Skerries and hookers from Galway and Kinsale fished off Kerry, detailed nets used, and listed catching of mackerel and pilchards as well as herring. He urged the erection of a lighthouse on Valentia Island. O'Brien sent his report to the RDS; full of interesting facts and practical suggestions, it shows the fishing industry struggling doggedly to survive with no encouragement from above, and demonstrates once more that every generation of Irishmen had produced optimists with reasoned hopes for the industry's future.

Between 1801 and 1810 herring exports were worth only £2,000 a year on average, a 50 per cent decrease on the previous decade, which was itself dismally worse than the one before. But other fish were being caught and it seems likely that in Dublin at least the consumption of fish was considerable in the early 1800s. There were said to be eighty-seven boats fishing out of County Dublin ports then, employing over 600 men, and the celebrated Dublin Bay herring boat was evolving. A print of 1799 in the Gilman Collection in Dun Laoghaire shows a fishing wherry in the poor fishing haven of Old Dunleary. Eighteen years later, to Rennie's design, the great artificial port of Dun Laoghaire (Kingstown for a century from 1821) was begun, long to be the world's largest artificial harbour. By the 1830s there were twenty fishing yawls registered in the port and the fishing out of it was so good that Cornish fishermen poured in. (It was they who at this period founded the still flourishing Methodist Church in Dun Laoghaire.)

The British investigator Wakefield calculated that there were 9,911 Irish fishermen operating in 1811. He claimed that 'the only boats used at present consist merely of a wooden frame, covered with a horse's or a bullock's hide'. This, however, contradicts the figure given by other observers that around that time some 400 Kinsale hookers of up to 20 tons were fishing. Wakefield was perhaps referring specially to the

A view of the new pier and lighthouse at Howth, 1817. Howth was an important fishing port already early in the last century.

LXVI. And for the Encouragement of the Coast Fisheries of *Ireland*, be it enacted, That it shall and may be lawful for the Lord Lieutenant, or other Chief Governor or Governors of *Ireland*, from Time to Time to direct any Sum or Sums of Money not exceeding the Sum of Five thousand Pounds in any one Year, to be paid to the Commissioners of the *Irish* Fisheries, out of the Revenues of the Customs and Port Duties in *Ireland*, to be applied by the said Commissioners in the Encouragement of such Coast Fisheries, under such Orders, Rules, Regulations, and Directions, as the said Commissioners shall from Time to Time think fit to make for that Purpose: Provided always, that the said Commissioners shall, on or before the First Day of *June* in each Year, report to the Lord Lieutenant, or other Chief Governor or Governors of *Ireland* for the Time being, in what Manner and under what Regulations such Sum or Sums of Money have been applied; and that a Copy of such Report signed by the said Commissioners shall from Time to Time be laid before both Houses of Parliament, within Fourteen Days after the Commencement of every Session next ensuing such First Day of *June*.

Lord Lieutenant may order Money to be paid out of the Revenue of Customs to the Commissioners of the Fisheries, for the Encouragement of the Coast Fisheries.

Extract from a Statute of George IV, 1819 establishing an Irish Fisheries Board and the introduction of a £5,000 grant, annually to the fishing industry

herring fishery which, according to Barne's *Statistical Account of Ireland* of 1811, had 'declined greatly since 1785; but cod, ling and hake are in as great abundance as ever'. As late as 1810 herrings were being caught in quantities off Achill and there were at that time twenty-one fish-curing centres on our coasts.

In 1819 the absurd fact that Ireland had become a fish-importing rather than a fish-exporting country stirred the authorities into getting an act passed at Westminster establishing a new fishery board, and decreeing that £5,000 be provided annually for building suitable fishing boats and for curing. Extra grants were given for building piers and harbours and subsidies were again placed on exports. Inspectors were appointed to supervise the quality of herrings for export and to give instruction on fishing and curing methods. Seeing that the 'free' parliament had provided most of these facilities more than three decades earlier and that in the meantime they

had been withdrawn, while British fishermen had received their equivalent and while duties on salt and on timber for boat building were higher here than in the other island, this act was long overdue. It was in fact ungenerous and there were justified criticisms that only fishermen who already had capital could qualify for the subsidies for new boats. Yet, as always, immediately the smallest gesture was made in favour of the industry, it responded.

In 1821 there were 4,889 boats fishing out of Irish ports, employing 21,400 men and boys, but by 1829 these figures had risen to 12,611 and 63,400 and an amending act had been passed in 1824 allotting £500 yearly (far too little) for repairing poor fishermen's boats. The Repeal Association was later to issue an official report emphasising the prosperity of our sea fisheries in the 1820s after an official government report had declared in 1836 that 'under the operation of the system [set up by the 1819 act] a great increase

Appendix, No. 7.

AN ACCOUNT of the Annual Fund of £.5,000 late Currency, or £.4,615. 7 *s.* 8 *d.* present Currency, granted to the Commissioners of the Irish Fisheries, pursuant to the Act of the 59th Geo. 3, c. 109, s. 66, and of all Sums contributed in aid of said Fund for one year ; from the 5th April 1828 to the 5th April 1829.—And of the Engagements of the Board to the same period.

CHARGE:

	£.	s.	d.
Balance in the Bank of Ireland on the 5th of April 1828, as appears by the Ninth Report of the Commissioners to Parliament - - - - -	19,040	11	10
Sum of £.5,000, late currency, lodged in the Bank of Ireland ; the grant for the year ended the 5th April 1829 - - - - - - - - -	4,615	7	8

PRIVATE CONTRIBUTION IN AID OF PIERS :

Counties.	Piers.		£.	s.	d.		£.	s.	d.
Antrim -	- Portmuck	- from William McClelland, esq. -	110	—	—				
Cork - -	- Glandore	- from Christopher Allen, esq. - -	40	—	—				
Clare - -	- Liscannor	- from Sir Augustine Fitzgerald - -	132	—	—				
Down -	- Newcastle	- from the Earl Annesley - - -	2,300	—	—				
Kerry -	- Kenmare	- from the Marquis of Lansdowne -	324	—	—				
Waterford { Wyse's Point / Ballinacourty }		from Thomas Wyse, esq. and local subscription - - - -	350	—	—				
		Total amount of Private Contribution - - -					3,256	—	—

IRISH FISHERY LOAN FUND, MISCELLANEOUS RECEIPTS.

Repayment of Loans :

Districts.			£.	s.	d.		£.	s.	d.
Sligo - -	- from Edward Nicholson, local inspector, in payment of fishermen's promissory notes passed for new boats, and for the repairs and supplies of boats - - - -		279	18	11				
Killybegs -	from Richd W. Nesbitt, local inspector		383	18	11				
Rathmullen,	from Samuel Robinson - -	d° -	8	—	—				
Belfast - -	from Arch^d MacDougall -	- d° -	112	—	7				
Ardglass -	from Henry Pentland -	- d^o -	561	12	10				
Carlingford,	from Francis J. Turner - -	d° -	485	7	6				
Balbriggan,	from H. J. Johnson - - -	d° -	358	2	6				
Dublin - -	- from James Irvine - -	d° -	403	17	—				
Wexford -	- from Edward Church -	- d^o -	384	12	—				
Dungarvan,	from Richard Dodd - -	d° -	149	16	6				
Valentia -	- from George Woodhouse -	- d° -	271	7	9				
Kinsale - -	from Malachy Donellan -	- d• -	248	13	6				
Glandore -	from Lyttleton Lyster -	- d• -	234	5	—				
Baltimore -	from Thomas Townsend -	- d• -	118	7	4				
Bantry -	- from James O. B. Croker -	- d^o -	379	15	3				
Dingle - -	from George Woodhouse -	- d° -	476	9	9				
Kilrush -	- from James Paterson -	- d° -	17	1	4				
Galway -	from Henry Cashel - -	d° -	504	3	5				
Clifden - -	from John MacDonnell -	- d• -	316	3	9				
Westport -	from Francis Kenny - -	d° -	388	11	6				
							6,082	5	4

The account of the annual grant of £5,000 to the fishing industry as reported in the Tenth Report of the Commissioners of the Irish Fishery Office, 1829

Appendix, No. 1. - - - - - - -

AN ACCOUNT of the Number of Decked VESSELS, Half-decked Vessels, Open Sail Boats, Row Boats, Total employed in Gutting and Packing, Number of Coopers, Number of Sail-makers, Number of Net-makers, and the

DISTRICTS and STATIONS.	Decked Vessels.			Half-decked Vessels.			Open Sail Boats.	
	No.	Tonnage	Men.	No.	Tonnage.	Men.	No.	Men.
Northern. Belfast	15	275	67	27	294	121	327	1,209
Rathmullen	Nil.	Nil.	Nil.	Nil.	Nil.	Nil.	19	83
Sligo	4	71	25	8	57	40	41	246
Killybegs	Nil.	Nil.	Nil.	Nil.	Nil.	Nil.	Nil.	Nil.
Eastern. Ardglass	39	1,128	245	93	1,113	546	63	338
Dublin	59	2,066	366	10	268	57	245	1,470
Balbriggan	85	2,433	509	4	80	22	-	-
Carlingford	21	695½	154	21	495	147	10	50
Wexford	Nil.	Nil.	Nil.	76	711½	380	396	2,137
Southern. Bantry	7	163	42	4	57	20	57	285
Baltimore	5	125½	29	27	445½	143	49	221
Dungarvan	81	1,601	567	26	297	140	17	75
Glandore	10	317	100	18	281	134	16	123
Kinsale	5	110	30	160	2,098	843	45	231
Valentia	-	-	-	4	$36\frac{16}{94}$	21	106	742
Dingle	1	16	3	28	226½	141	203	1,364
Western. Westport	7	147	38	20	175	81	116	393
Galway	12	281	59	6	111	30	484	2,420
Clifden	-	-	-	16	206	48	167	501
Kilrush	2	64	12	163	1,467	652	12	48
Totals - - -	353	9,493	2,246	711	8,518	3,566	2,373	11,936

Irish Fishery Office,⎫
  Dublin.   ⎬
           ⎭

H. Townsend.

A census of fishing boats taken from the Tenth Report of the Commissioners of the Irish Fishery Office, 1829 (see p. 55 also)

Appendix, No. 1.

Number of Fishermen employed, Number of Curing Houses, Number of Men employed therein, Number of Men Total Number of Fishermen and Tradesmen employed in the IRISH FISHERIES; for the year ended 5th April 1829.

Row Boats. No.	Row Boats. Men.	Total Number of Fishermen employed.	Fish Curers. No. of Curing Houses.	Fish Curers. No. of Men employed in them.	Number of Persons employed in Gutting and Packing.	Coopers: Number of them.	Sail Makers: Number of them.	Net Makers: Number of them.	Total Number of Fishermen and Tradesmen employed in the Irish Fisheries.
96	669	2,066	Nil.	Nil.	120	110	27	66	2,389
464	2,355	2,438	10	11	Nil.	6	The fishermen make their own sails and nets.		2,455
532	3,192	3,503	43	132	300	Nil.	8	2,028	5,971
723	3,882	3,882	12	24	-	-	-	-	3,906
306	2,224	3,353	20	uncertain.	uncertain.	21	4	200	3,578
29	140	2,033	Nil.	Nil.	Nil.	Nil.	Nil.	Nil.	2,033
58	332	863	Nil.	Nil.	Nil.	Nil.	5	Nil.	868
440	2,206	2,557	8	Nil.	Nil.	Many coopers in the district but none employed in the fishery.	3 but most all fishermen make their own sails.	Between men women and children about 700 in the season.	3,260
-	-	2,517	-	-	-	-	-	-	2,517
635	3,265	3,612	37	74	148	20	10	100	3,964
351	1,958	2,351	*398	Same as in gutting & packing.	1,056	-	1	276	3,693
260	1,040	1,822	None.	Each person cures his own fish in his house	Nil.	4	3	Every one of the fishermen make their own nets.	1,829
555	3,419	3,776	*599	1,797	Included in account of curers.	8	6	Included in account of curers.	5,587
662	3,508	4,612	210	1,282	-	120	13	500	6,527
183	1,025	1,788	Nil.	Nil.	Nil.	Nil.	Nil.	Nil.	1,788
21	72	1,580	Nil.	Nil.	Nil.	Nil.	Nil.	Nil.	1,580
1,000	4,436	4,948	There are no regular curing houses in this district; the herrings are cured in bulk, and ungutted. Same applies to sail and net makers, the fishermen making the latter. For larger vessels English canvas is used; for smaller boats, bandle linen made in the country.						4,948
1,199	4,796	7,305	23	394	460	27	4	600	8,700
1,235	5,459	6,008	-	30	-	-	-	Supposed 400	6,438
425	1,695	2,407	No established curing houses.	Cured by the fishermen & families.	-	Very few herrings cured now for bounty.	40 Fishermen make their own sails.	Made by the women, who may amount to 5,000.	2,447
9,174	45,673	63,421	1,360	3,654	2,094	316	121	4,770	74,478

The fishermen of these districts have a small chamber attached to most of their dwelling houses, in which they cure their fish. The officers have therefore returned them as *curing-houses*.

in the activity of the trade was experienced, much capital was drawn to it, and large sums were circulated amongst the fishermen and curers'. By 1829 export subsidies were claimed on 41,633 barrels of fish compared with 16,855 in 1824. In 1830, however, this legislation, under which the subsidies decreased annually in amount, was let lapse altogether.

Our fishing industry was the victim of government high-handedness, dictated by 'laissez faire' economic theory, just when it was getting back on its feet. A commission appointed in 1835 to report on the sharp decline which the industry was by then experiencing recommended that aid for pier and harbour construction be resumed, that the Board of Works be authorised to advance half the cost of building roads leading to fishing centres, curing stations, salt houses and fishermen's dwellings, and that the government should provide educational facilities regarding fishing.

This report was ignored and although the Board of Works was appointed the authority for regulating and controlling the industry in 1842, it was given no money to spend on its promotion. The government's behaviour, motivated in part in all likelihood by a vague fear that a growing industry here would threaten the one in Britain, is of course one of the reasons why the considerable proportion of our people fishing in the 'Hungry Forties' were able to contribute so little to combatting the spreading hunger. It is why Davis was writing in *The Nation* of the great opportunities for developing our fisheries and demanding the provision of adequate fishing harbours.

Meanwhile in the 1820s 'bag nets' and 'stake nets' had been introduced for the capture of salmon which one authority, S.P. Digby in an issue of *The Bell*, describes, providing evidence, as 'the

common food of the people' in Munster. These instruments, legalised in 1842, superseded the traditional drift nets and brush head weirs. Sites for their erection were let by land-owners indiscriminately, the traditional fishermen were largely ruined and the former abundance of stock reduced, and never in fact restored. The estimated 2,000 salmon fishermen working the Waterford estuary in the traditional local craft, the cot, were reduced to beggary after harsh repression by police and military of the raids they very naturally made on the instruments that were ruining them. This is one more example of authority's neglect of the interests of fisheries and fishermen during this sombre period. The Fishery Board in Scotland, which was not suppressed, prevented any such depletion of stocks there. It was calculated before Ardnacrusha was built in the 1920s that the Shannon produced only one fish per superficial acre of catchment area to the Scottish Tay's six.

After a decline of more than 30 per cent up to 1836 in the number of boats fishing following the dissolution of the Fishery Board of 1819, population pressure forced more men to sea. By 1845 some 4,700 more boats were operating than nine years earlier. Over 100 boats were working from Arklow alone in this period, fishing for herring and oysters. The Devon Commission of 1844 had emphasised the valuable work done by the Fishery Board of 1819–30 and deplored the lack of capital which prevented a willing population of fishermen from equipping themselves with adequate boats (reckoned to cost about £300) for going out to fish. Curing stations, which the fishermen had no resources to run themselves, were now non-existent; salt, no longer taxed, was nevertheless kept by merchants at an artificially high price; and in many western coastal areas herrings were used

1. The Leader.
2. The Entrance into the Chamber.
3. The Circular Chamber.

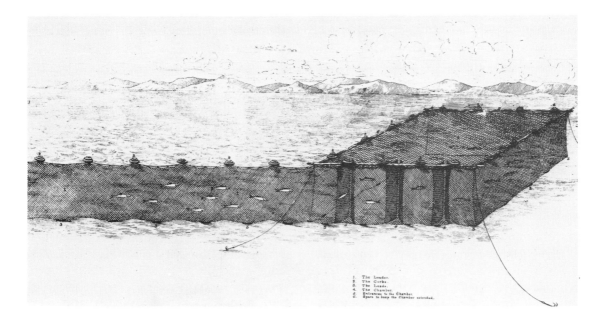

1. The Leader.
2. The Corks.
3. The Leads.
4. The Chamber.
5. Entrances to the Chamber.
6. Spars to keep the Chamber extended.

Salmon nets in use in the mid nineteenth century. Top: *a stake net;* bottom: *a bag net*

A Limerick cot. Reproduced from Ireland: its scenery and character *by Mr. and Mrs. S. C. Hall, 1845*

for manure. All this while famine was about to strike and while the same Westminster parliament which ignored the claims of our fisheries was generously subsidising those in Scotland. (In 1850 Ireland was Scotland's chief market for fish.)

The Earl of Glengall's letter to the Devon Commission, printed by George O'Brien in his *Economic History*, deserves quotation: 'The truth is, an intrigue to destroy the Irish deep sea fisheries was too successful, in order that (as I believe) the Scotch fisheries might not be interfered with; and this just at the moment that the Board (of 1819) had seen their way through their difficulties.' In 1844 the Board of Works even refused a £5,000 loan offered by a London society for advancing money to legitimate Irish fishermen borrowers. Shipbuilding also languished here. Fewer ships were built in Ireland in 1849 (25) than in 1794 (35), and though there had been a revolution in shipbuilding elsewhere

boosting the size of ships, the tonnage built in 1849 (2,147) was only 706 above that of fifty-five years before.

It must be admitted that the shock of the Famine did cause some belated steps to be taken to help our fishermen to improve their own lot and contribute to the needs of the country, now so urgent. An act was passed in 1846 authorising the grant of £50,000 for building piers and harbours, but on condition that the county, district or landlord on whose land the improvement was carried out paid 25 per cent of the cost. In 1847, £40,000 was voted for the same purpose and £68,636 in 1850. The 1846 act also enabled seven model fish curing stations to be set up — at Roundstone, Baltimore, Castletown, Valentia, Inniscoe, Killybegs and Belmullet. Though these were soon closed, private enterprise had taken the hint and a number of privately-owned curing stations was opened and struggled on.

In 1848 Wallop Brabazon published a

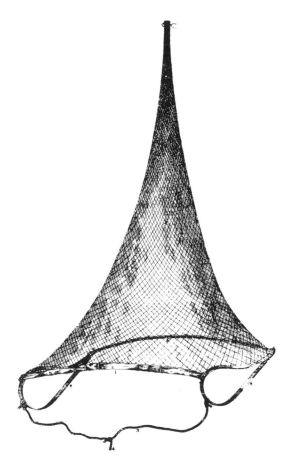

A trawl net in use in the mid nineteenth century

pamphlet, *The Deep Sea and Coast Fisheries of Ireland, with suggestions for the Working of a Fishing Company.* Whether in hope or in irony he dedicated his finely illustrated work to the Commissioners of Public Works. He attributed the decline of the fishing industry essentially to the withdrawal of subsidies after 1830. He also advocated the very far-seeing idea of a fixed minimum price for fish, 'so that the poor fishermen might have some benefit out of a large take of fish, instead of dreading a glut for fear of seeing fish left to rot on the beach for want of a market'. Another demand of his was for the introduction of a type of vessel that could be used in the off-season to export cargoes of cured fish and import cargoes of salt. More important, he cited the fishermen of Skerries as successfully surviving through hard times by use of the plans he was proposing.

So at the beginning of this dark epoch in Irish history we find fishing prospering, in spite of governmental indifference and general decline, in places like Kinsale, Rush, Dun Laoghaire, Kenmare and the Waterford estuary, and Charles O'Brien suggesting practical moves for improving the industry in the south-west. At the end of it there were still fishing communities like that of Skerries that could rise above the tide of misery by intelligence and concerted effort, and Wallop Brabazon was advancing far-seeing projects for revival of the industry at its very moment of collapse.

These islands were on the brink of a revolution in fish consumption, the railway and the ice plant putting fresh fish within reach of millions who had hitherto eaten it only cured. And there was still enough resilience in the bitterly-tried Irish fishing community, and still enough faith here and there in the enlightened public, for hope to remain alive, that one day Ireland would have prosperous fisheries guided by scientific methods.

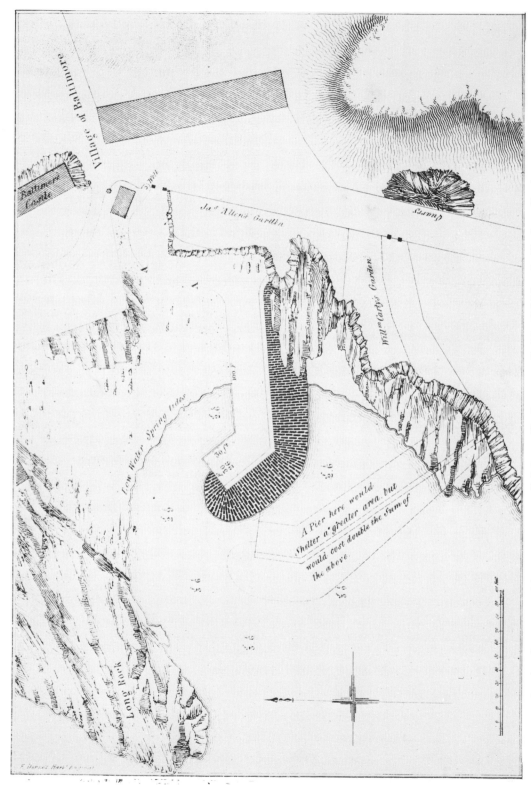

The plan for proposed improvements to Baltimore Harbour supplied in 1826 by the Harbour Engineer for Ireland

6

Ireland's Sea Fisheries from the Famine to Arthur Griffith

The years between the Famine and the establishment of a separate Irish state saw many fluctuations in the condition of the industry. They also saw, very gradually, the application of scientific research and a rudimentary measure of planning in the industry; spasmodically, attention was paid to the opinions of some of the fishermen themselves. Lack of capital, however, continued to be the most formidable obstacle to the industry's growth. It was the more crippling because this was the age that saw the foreign fishing fleets that have habitually fished our waters turn from sail to steam. But the last years of the period also saw the perennial optimism of what remained of the traditional hardcore fishing community compounded by two developments. One was the construction at Arklow of a revolutionary fishing craft, the *Ovoca*, the first motor fishing vessel built in these islands. The other was Arthur Griffith's expressed conviction that an independent Ireland would thrive as much by ex-

Fishing craft leaving Kingstown Harbour, 1842

ploitation of her vast fishing potential as by the continuing development of the agricultural economy. And Griffith was one of those who epitomised the new, twentieth-century Irish national movement.

Between 1861 and 1865 there were still 10,713 craft fishing from our shores, operated by 45,839 men and boys. The average for the next five-year period was down to 9,265 boats and 39,274 crew and between 1871 and 1875 the average was 7,472 boats and 29,860 crew. Between 1876 and 1890, with the population steadily falling, the industry stabilised with just over 22,000 fishing from some 5,800 boats. Though the revolutionary steam trawler had now made its appearance, **the Irish fisherman was still** fishing from a small sailing craft. By 1910, when Arthur Griffith was striving to impress awakening Ireland with the vast possibilities in fishing, the population engaged in the industry was somewhat under 21,000 — a higher proportion of the total population than in the closing years of the previous century — with somewhat larger boats. The industry was putting up a brave fight. It was not till the shameful neglect of the first two decades under the separate Irish state that the fishing population began to look as if it might disappear altogether. It was down to 7,351 on the eve of the second World War.

Two perennial weaknesses of the Irish fishing industry, which it has not yet wholly shed, were that for many inshore

A trawler with her trawl down. Taken from The Deep Sea and Coast Fisheries of Ireland *by Wallop Brabazon, 1848*

fishermen this occupation was only ancillary to farming, and the number of shore jobs it generated was ludicrously low. Arthur Reynolds, the distinguished editor of *The Irish Skipper*, writing in 1963, reckoned that a modern centralised fishing industry should provide six jobs ashore for every fisherman afloat (the Irish fishing industry has a long way to go still to achieve this). In 1829, one of the best years of the Fishery Board, there were only 11,000 working ashore in conjunction with the 64,771 afloat. Another weakness (now being overcome) was the migratory nature of Irish fishing, boats moving from tiny port to tiny port following the shoals, without any real base. This weakened arguments put up to less than sympathetic authorities for money to be spent to improve fishing ports. These were often too shallow and unprotected from storms from nearly all directions; this was one of many factors militating against the acquisition by fishermen of bigger boats.

The normal small boat was vulnerable, and losses of fishermen at sea were disproportionately high as is grimly shown in the lifeboat station records of the nineteenth-century held by the Maritime Institute at Dun Laoghaire. Sometimes fishing fleets were wrecked beyond repair in some inadequate harbour — it happened three times at Kilmore Quay, where a single storm once smashed no fewer than twenty fishing craft. Wexford fishermen suffered particularly severely, as the celebrated ballad of the Faythe fishing fleet recalls. This refers to a disaster of 1833. But all acquainted with Synge's masterly *Riders to the Sea* will know that the fisherman's life was indeed precarious in the long centuries between the Tudor conquest and the awakening of national consciousness to the importance of fisheries, less than twenty years ago.

Arthur Griffith's arguments to convince the awakening nation that its future lay with an expanding fishing industry did not arise out of a vacuum. Long before, the establishment of the Congested Districts Board in 1891 reflected a long overdue, if casual, re-awakening of official interest in fishing; at least in the West a fairly consistent chorus had been audible in certain intellectual circles demanding the elaboration and implementation of a central fishery policy. Publications such as the *Dublin University Magazine, The Irish Quarterly Review* and *The Irish Builder,* RDS bulletins and a number of pamphlets raised the fisheries issue in cogent terms. Unfortunately, the writers, if persuasive enough to keep the issue alive, were not influential enough to rattle authority. The intellectuals of 1850—1900, however, compare most favourably with those of the first generation of the separate Irish state. These almost unanimously turned their backs on the national maritime heritage and made it impossible for the ordinary citizen to remember we even had one. It is a sombre commentary on the Irish education system that after the state was set up, and the almost coincidental death of the champion of a national fisheries policy, no individual of any consequence and no organisation appeared for nearly two decades to re-echo the call Griffith had been making in the early years of the century.

Let us now examine what the *Dublin University Magazine* was propagating in 1851 and 1852. A long article in the issue for November 1851 was entitled 'The salmon and sea fisheries'. The first half of the article analysed the disastrous condition of the salmon fisheries since 1842; it produced evidence to show that catches had fallen off in every single region of the country, and the writer stated that salmon production in the country had fallen by as much as 66 per cent since 1841. Turning to the sea

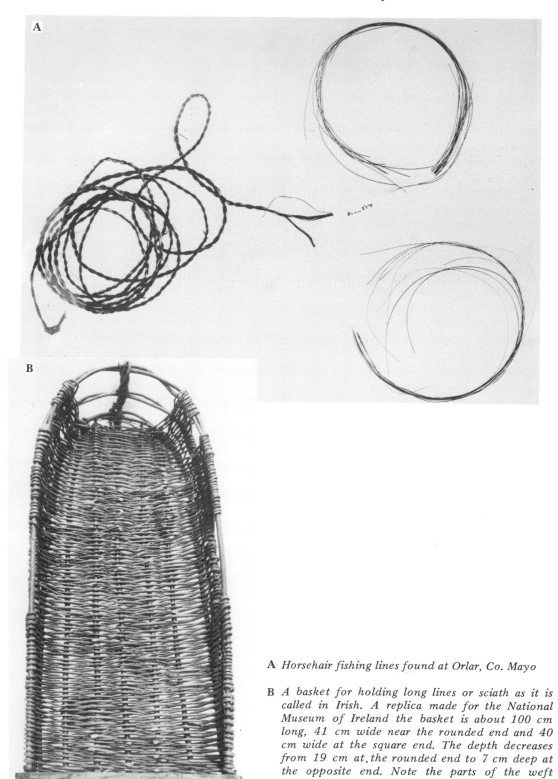

A *Horsehair fishing lines found at Orlar, Co. Mayo*

B *A basket for holding long lines or sciath as it is called in Irish. A replica made for the National Museum of Ireland the basket is about 100 cm long, 41 cm wide near the rounded end and 40 cm wide at the square end. The depth decreases from 19 cm at the rounded end to 7 cm deep at the opposite end. Note the parts of the weft left vacant to form handles for carrying the basket*

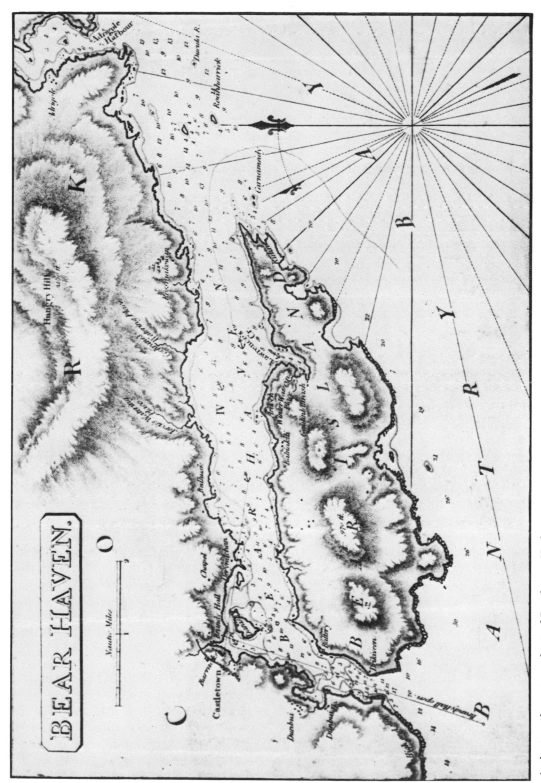

A nineteenth century chart of Berehaven Harbour

Commons had reported in 1849 in no uncertain terms that it believed that the Irish salmon fisheries at least must be transferred at once to a separate department. This is declared to be 'absolutely necessary'; still nothing was done.

The 1852 article went on to recapitulate the arguments of the 1851 one, and expressed astonishment that Howth, so close to Dublin, was not a prosperous fishing port. Once more, allusion is made to the encouragement received by the Scottish fisheries in the form of substantial government grants. A strong call is also made for the creation of an Irish fishery protection patrol to prevent poaching and too large concentrations of fishing craft in one spot. Time, of course, has proved the wisdom of this call, and the author of 1852 would no doubt be delighted to see the fishery protection activities of today's expanding Irish naval service.

In 1856 *The Irish Quarterly Review* published an article 'Irish fisheries', a summary of a series of recent proposals on the topic published by a Dublin barrister, Robert Worthington. One of the first points Worthington made was that salmon had become 'a dish almost unknown to the poor', a reminder again that before the last century salmon was commonly eaten by nearly every family in the country. The act of 1842 was once again castigated, above all for its destruction of traditional salmon rights and its delivery of this fishery into the hands of profiteers and speculators.

Rather typically, the article ends by asserting that all that was wanting to restore our fisheries to their former prosperity was 'a good law, properly administered', which 'befitting energy' could win. It is as true today as it was then that the fishing industry needs good legislation to guide it. But what Robert Worthington and a host of other well-intentioned theoreticians, before him and since, have missed, is the indispensability of active consultation with the fishermen themselves and their co-operation in order to make the law work. It is only in our own day that this marriage of theory and practice has become a possibility. It is now more indispensable than ever that scientists, administrators, skippers and deckhands should be welded into a single unit for the advancement of the industry.

In 1866 *The Irish Quarterly Review* took a long look at various comments recently published about a pamphlet by a British naval officer, Captain T.E. Symonds, managing director of the London and West of Ireland Fishing and Fish Manure Company. Reference was made to an English North Sea fishery expert who had visited Bantry in 1855 and 'literally rowed across that fine bay through a bank of herrings'. He maintained that if the Irish fishermen operating there that night had had nets like the Manx and Cornishmen they would have taken 40,000 barrels. By 1866, however, some administrative reforms had been effected and the Irish fisheries were now under the control of a special Commissioner of Irish Fisheries. Under his direction it had been established (once more!) that the seas round Ireland had a superabundance of fish in them. In Clew Bay alone, thirty-three types of fish were to be found, in addition to whelks and lug, scallops, crabs, lobsters, oysters, crawfish and other shellfish, basking sharks, seals and angel sharks, not to mention carrigeen moss, seaweed for manure or kelp, samphire and shell-sand. An important stage had in fact been attained in the scientific evaluation of our maritime resources; the next step would be to embark on a national exploitation of them. (Ireland was at the time importing £200,000 worth of Scottish herring a year.)

Symonds was convinced this could be done. He believed that Galway, with a fishing population of 7,794 in and around its bay working 1,811 boats, should have 'one of the most flourishing fisheries of Europe', supplying Dublin within six hours and Birmingham within eighteen. (Railways had spread to most parts of Ireland since the Famine.) His company was about to invest £30,000 for the development of Galway Bay fisheries, using vessels of 75—80 tons, some with wells to keep fish, lobsters and bait alive, drifters of 25—30 tons, long-liners, 30—35-foot row-boats for seining, a steam schooner for transporting fish, a curing station, a smoking house, a fish-oil works and ice-houses. It was intended to convert coarse fish 'of an unsaleable abundance' into fish manure, the great value of which had recently been established in France. Symonds spoke highly of the Claddagh fishermen, and discounted legends of their unruliness.

Efforts such as this, even if spasmodic and often ephemeral, combined with the dogged perserverence of the hard-core fishing population (whose views however were still not consulted), helped to stabilise the industry in the decades to come, though still at an unacceptably low level.

On 19 February, 1866 the chairman of the Natural History and Museum Department of the RDS, William Andrews, MRIA, read before his Society a paper entitled 'The herring fisheries of Ireland'. Once again the value of the 1819 Act was stressed (Andrews went so far as to state that just before its

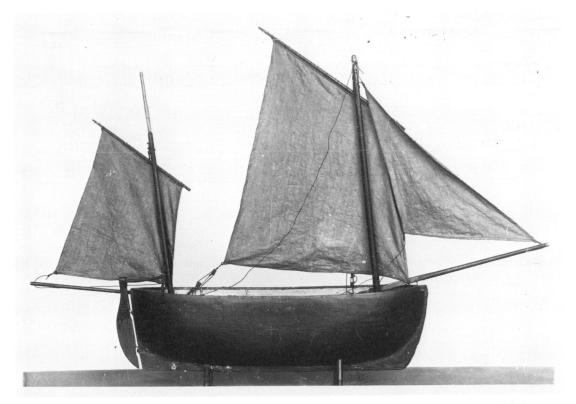

Alleged to be a model of a Dublin Bay herring boat, similar to a Mounts Bay lugger with jib on a bow-sprit and mizen rigged boomkin (second half of nineteenth century)

enactment the fishing population had shrunk to only 188, a figure not easily credible). Under this Act a brig of 78 tons and sloops of 55 to 67 tons had been fishing; when it lapsed, the larger fishing vessels vanished. 'Still, however, there were enterprising factors who annually fitted out vessels for the purchase of herrings round the coasts. . . and the wherries and smacks of Skerries and Rush occasionally made their north-west visits for cod to Boffin *and even to Iceland*' (present author's emphasis). Herring were still fished from Killybegs, Galway and Bantry.

William Andrews then went on to give his explanation why the Scottish fisheries had not declined while ours had, though both lost their subsidies in 1830. The Scottish fishermen had superior nets and other gear and they also had a better education. As recently as 1861 there had been only four boats fishing out of Howth but by 1866, Andrews declared, a real revival had occurred 'and the men of Howth, Skerries, Balbriggan and Arklow can vie with the ablest of the Cornish and Scottish craft'. At Skerries there were now 116 smacks and luggers, some of 30 tons, with full complements of herring nets. Kinsale was also thriving. Andrews attributed the great improvement to the activities of a body charmingly named 'The Society for Bettering the Condition of the Poor in Ireland'. This Society was advancing loans (they totalled only £3,000 annually), free of interest, with easy instalment repayments. A Balbriggan fisherman had told Andrews he had made 30 per cent on the loan he had got.

William Andrews went on to make a number of observations about the life-span and habits of the herring, about which he admitted science was still ignorant (do we yet know all we should about the Irish herring?). One recent October, 400,000 herring had been taken in one day at Oranmore and brought to Galway market; Andrews, however, advocated a closed season for herring catching (in November and December, and from mid-February to mid-April). Had Andrews's suggestions that there should be more research and, on the basis of this research, certain seasonal restrictions, been followed, our fisheries would have profited greatly. Andrews also noted that recent improvements in east coast herring catches had revived demands for a return to the branding system in force under the 'free' parliament so as to guarantee quality.

Andrews, moreover, maintained that a parliamentary grant for the Irish fisheries had been deliberately withheld by the government in London for the past thirty-five years. He also raised again the perennial demand for more capital for the industry, larger boats, and reconstructed harbours. He pointed out that charts of the ports were inadequate, and that there was no port of refuge for fishing craft between Dun Laoghaire and Ardglass to the north and Wexford to the south, a very serious matter now that the east coast fisheries were progressing and employing larger vessels. He proposed a radical reconstruction of Skerries harbour. (In fact as far back as 1856 the British House of Commons had formally considered a voluminous report on the desirability of a harbour of refuge at Skerries but, as with so many propositions for improvements in Ireland, no action was taken.) Andrews also propounded a theory that was far ahead of the times, namely that training ships should be commissioned at various points round the coast to ensure an improvement in understanding of fishing problems and techniques. Once again, here was a project which, had it been put into practice, would vastly have benefited our fishing industry.

Lively discussion followed Andrews' RDS paper. All who spoke agreed that there had been a noteworthy revival of our fisheries in recent years. In particular, Matthew McGowan of Skerries (Master Mariner) said that he thoroughly agreed with William Andrews in all his views and remarks on the fisheries around the coast of Ireland. McGowan spoke from an experience of seventeen years, having fished all the principal grounds of the north-west and west coasts, especially off Innisboffin, and also off the south coast, and along the entire east coast; he had also been with his vessel to Iceland. He fully agreed with Andrews about harbours and their present state:

A proper investigation of their present condition, and of their insecurity and unsuitability to large-class fishing boats, is absolutely essential to a proper promotion of the fisheries. Skerries, in particular, is almost useless, from the shoaling of the best parts of the harbour, from the large quantities of ballast that have for years past been discharged there, not unfrequently, as Mr. Andrews has observed, 150 tons in the week. The large assemblage of English, Scotch, and Manx fishing boats that annually frequent Skerries would be greatly benefited by an extension of the harbour, as proposed by Mr. Andrews, not to speak of the large and increasing numbers of Irish boats that are throughout the year there. Besides, the localities of the fishing grounds are such, that great loss of time occurs in working to and from Howth with contrary winds. The improvement to Skerries, suggested by Mr. Andrews, would with strong easterly gales afford great shelter to all classes of vessels, as much damage in such weather too frequently happens along the east coast. At the Isle of Man, at St. Ives, at Wick, and at other fishing stations on the British coasts, good safety harbours have been formed; and, although petitions have been signed in favour of Skerries by English and Scotch fishermen, by those from Cumberland, Whitehaven, and Maryport, and also by the Drogheda Commissioners, there is no Member of Parliament to advocate our cause, nor Fishery Commissioners to report to Government in our behalf as in Scotland, when we have had 500 sail in our road in the fishing season. Much more could be represented, but Mr. Andrews has fully advanced all that could be said on the subject.

It is interesting to note that it was an Irishman, Musgrave, who between 1860 and 1870 made the first experiments in the use of the otter board, by far the most effective method of keeping towed nets open horizontally. This was a revolutionary Irish contribution to the development of the techniques of sea fishing. According to Andres van Brandt in *Fish Catching Methods of the World* (published 1964 by Fishing News Books Ltd.) The otter board for the trawl net in its present form appeared first in Ireland "around 1885." An English trawler experimented with otter boards in that year, but it was several years before sufficient experience had been acquired for the then flourishing British North Sea trawler fleets to feel justified in generally adopting the otter board.

In the 1870s and 1880s a persistent and admirably well-informed campaign in favour of developing our fisheries was carried on by an unlikely journal, *The Irish Builder*. Every aspect of the industry was examined in a series of cogent and well-researched articles. One of these on 1 January 1883 outlined the picturesque history of the Claddagh fishing community in the nineteenth century, ending very aptly with these words: 'An oil painting of the Claddagh fishermen at home on their native strand [there was apparently one on the walls of the Royal Hibernian Academy, J.deC.I] may be a very pretty and picturesque sight, but we prefer to see the Claddagh and other Irish fishermen manning large, well-built, and fully-equipped boats, and fleets constantly going out and returning with the rich harvests of the sea, which are inexhaustible'.

The Irish Builder, which frequently complained that it was fighting a lone battle, was particularly critical of the poor state of our fishing harbours. Over and over again, like other critics before and since but with exceptional perserverance and force, it castigated authority for its neglect in this domain; it repeated the old message that we could never take full advantage of our unique situation surrounded by swarming fishing grounds, until we had ports and piers to service an up-to-date fishing fleet.

The Irish Builder of 15 July, 1880 in a leader headed 'The industrial bearings of our fisheries' quoted the chief secretary for Ireland, William Edward Brown known as "Buckshot" Forster, on our fisheries. What he said rejecting a call for government financial aid for our fisheries casts a lurid light on the reasons why these were neglected in the last century by the government of the day; the 'laissez faire' or 'survival of the fittest' theory dominated economic thought and practice almost throughout the world. (Even if Ireland had achieved a home rule government in the 1880s it is questionable whether it would have done any more for our fisheries than the Westminster government did. Who except Michael Davitt

and perhaps J.J. O'Kelly among leading home rulers had the vision to see beyond the stifling economic dogma of the time? Did not all the early governments we had after the establishment of our separate state also accept by and large the same dogma and neglect our fisheries to an equal extent?)

It was in 1888 that steam trawlers began to operate in Wales from Cardiff and Milford, inaugurating half a century of scintillating profits for the fishing industry a few miles across the sea from us — an industry which had experienced much the same sort of history as ours up until then. In the 1870s and early 1880s the Welsh fishing industry had been in sharp decline: large quantities of Irish fish were being imported into Milford and Holyhead, and the prize essay on Welsh fisheries and how to develop them presented to the 1884 national eistedfodd emphasised that 'from Milford Haven to Holyhead, there is not a port into which a boat drawing eight feet six inches of water can run at all states of the tide', and 'as a trawling boat and fittings cost from £400 to £500, few people could afford this sum are willing. . . to invest it in hazardous undertaking'. The Welsh fisheries were transformed and vastly enriched by the arrival of the steam trawler. The steam trawler came to Wales, not through state intervention but because the country had huge resources in coal which were turned into vast profits through the exploitation of underpaid miners. Capital was available in floods to inaugurate new industries and re-energise old. This was the only way Forster and authority generally thought industries should be created; he said that any suggestion that fisheries or any industry should be carried on on state capital was unacceptable. We had no flourishing coal mines, and what little surplus capital was circulating in Ireland tended either

Howth Harbour with fishing craft (late nineteenth century)

to be exported or to be invested in quick-profit enterprises of far less national value than fisheries.

On 1 August, 1882 *The Irish Builder*, in an article on 'Royal harbours and fishery piers', remarked that the former mail packet station of Howth (unlike its favoured successor Dun Laoghaire — Kingstown) 'being now only a fishery harbour is not considered worth dredging'. What little the Board of Works did in Howth was an unavoidable minimum, without which 'the harbour would shortly disappear altogether'. The article derided 'the present cumbersome system' of getting harbours improved, either through the leaden-footed Board of Works or having to go 'to Westminster fighting a battle before a select committee, with a host of lawyers and witnesses fattening at the expense of this country'. Sixteen long years before elective county councils were finally introduced, the *Builder* was demanding them instead of the antique, landlord-dominated system of local government then operative. Elective county councils, the journal thought,

would show greater interest in fishery ports and act less dilatorily in improving them. In June 1882 the *Builder* had already complained that 'the action of the government is destroying the fishery trade on the east coast. . . . Howth is the central fishery station on the east coast but its harbour is neglected by the government'.

On 1 July 1883 the *Builder* returned to the same theme again. An international fisheries exhibition had just been held in London (the journal had been campaigning for ten Irish fishermen to attend it). The royal Duke of Edinburgh's paper on the fisheries of these islands had provided some useful Irish fishery statistics. The *Builder* commented: 'Practical action, however, must follow public utterance if our fisheries are to be developed, as no amount of mere Royal readings can effect much good'. One paper read at the exhibition made the very forward-looking suggestion that fishermen should be paid a basic minimum wage with a share of profits from the catch as bonus.

The article in *The Irish Builder* went on to quote Thomas F. Brady, Inspector of Irish Fisheries, who had been giving evidence on harbours before a House of Commons committee. This evidently conscientious and imaginative official's exasperation and impatience at the industry's dependence on the Board of Works gleams through the careful wording of his statements: 'There was not the slightest doubt that if two or three harbours were constructed the population (of the west) would be able to take advantage of them'; and as for Newcastle, County Down, 'the pier which had been built there at a cost of upwards of £10,000 had stood for a few years but got washed away'. Its harbour was now 'useless'. He had recommended the construction of seventy-one small harbours and piers after hearing local applications. The

Blessing the Claddagh fleet at the beginning of the fishing season. Reproduction from Irish Pictures Drawn with Pen and Pencil *by R. Lovett, 1888*

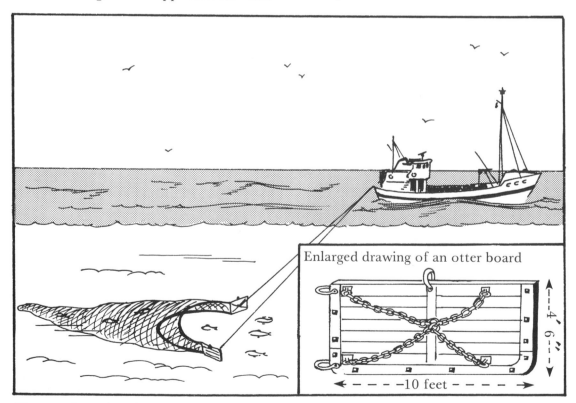

Enlarged drawing of an otter board

←- - - - 10 feet - - - - →

Diagram of otter boards

minimum cost 'according to the manner in which such harbours were built' would be £250,000. To do the work properly would require a lot more. All that was actually allocated by the treasury for the year was less than £4,000. The *Builder* once more urged reconstruction of Howth harbour, and suggested the establishment of a fish-curing station on Ireland's Eye.

Another article in the same issue of the *Builder* took the English journal *The Economist* to task for opposing the suggestion by Hugh Culling Bardley Childers, the distinguished member of Gladstone's Cabinet and for some years First Lord of the Admiralty — father of Erskine Childers of the *Asgard* and *The Riddle of the Sands* — that £250,000 ought to be found from funds available since the disestablishment of the Church of Ireland fourteen years before for

creating fishing harbours here. *The Economist* objected, on the old laissez faire grounds, to public money being spent to stimulate industry, which ought to be developed only by self-help. A fortnight later the *Builder* reopened the battle with an article 'Irish Harbour Accommodation and the Fisheries'. It supported a demand for new fishery harbours at Bantry bay, the Shannon estuary, Galway and Blacksod bays and Broadhaven, and referred again to Inspector Brady who had said that the Board of Works piers were 'perfectly useless for any improvement that might be contemplated'. On 1 May, 1885 the *Builder* once more wrote on 'Irish Fishery Piers and Harbours'. By then the £250,000 for Irish fishery harbours had at last been granted by the Westminster parliament; but the article pointed out that Belgium with (then)

Drying nets, Murlough Bay, Co. Antrim

much the same population as Ireland had spent £2,727,632 in six years on docks and harbours, and Holland with a million less people had spent £5,201,666 in twenty-one years.

In other articles the *Builder* repeatedly demonstrated that, as it remarked on 15 July, 1880, 'the development of the Irish fishery industry . . . means the development of various other industries, which would be the means of giving employment to several thousand artisans and sundry other workmen. Indeed, women, boys and girls, as well as men, would find profitable and constant employment'.

Although *The Irish Builder* admitted in its issue of 15 February 1876 that 'Ireland is awfully behind the sister kingdom in regard to her fisheries', and that the Isle of Man was curing four times as many herrings as Ireland, nevertheless it was evident that the fishermen of Ireland were despite all obstacles chalking up achievements. In just over a month in 1881, for instance, 1,000 tons of mackerel were caught off the Shannon estuary and exported to Britain, netting £40,000; this was incidentally a new mackerel fishery for the nineteenth century. Fifty to sixty fishing vessels were then working out of Foynes. In 1882, when it was calculated that only 5 per cent of Irish fishing vessels were 'first class', off Cork alone 100,000 boxes of mackerel were caught and exported to England for £128,500. And then there is this report from the Reverend C. Davis, parish priest of Baltimore, County Cork, printed in the *Builder* of 15 March 1881:

At present 26 fishing smacks, owned and manned by native fishermen hail from the port of Baltimore, and are now actively engaged every night in quest of mackerel. Each of these boats, with its train of nets, cost over £500. They are the same class of boats as are used by the Manx fishermen, having been all built in the Isle of Man. The crew consists of eight men, and the boats are necessarily much smaller than the French boats, as they must make rapid and daily runs into the narrow harbours of our coast to dispose of their fish. The fish is immediately purchased by English and Irish companies, packed into boxes, iced, and transmitted by rail or steamship to the English markets. In the island of Cape Clear, with a population of 540 souls, there were last year eight of these boats, and the crew of each realised during the season £500. There are this year 15 boats in the island. Some of them were purchased with the past earnings of the fishermen, but the greater number were obtained by the benevolent aid of Baroness Burdett-Coutts, who, within a short time, devoted the munificent sum of £5,000 for the purpose. I may observe that a very humble fisherman in Cape Clear has got, like the French, a donkey engine in his boat, for the purpose of hauling in his nets — the first instance of the kind, I believe, on record in an Irish fishing boat. There are also fishing boats, nearly all purchased in the Isle of Man, in the neighbouring island of Sherkin, in Glandore, Courtmacsherry, a large number in Kinsale, and, I believe, over 40 from the port of Dublin. There is no doubt a mine of wealth lies in the ocean that surrounds our island, and if properly worked and developed would bring comfort and even wealth to the very poorest of our countrymen. To my mind it is the most hopeful branch of national industry, if carefully fostered and encouraged. A few years ago the Reproductive Loan Fund was

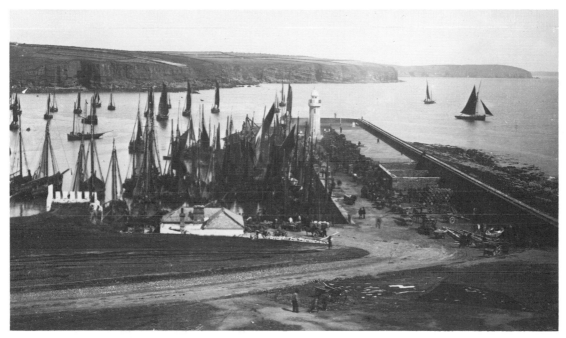

Dunmore, Co. Waterford. The herring fleet at the turn of the century

made available by way of loan to the fishermen of some counties of Ireland. But the largest sum allocated in any year was only £800, which would not purchase two of the boats I have been describing. A Bill was introduced into Parliament last session by Mr. Collins, member for Kinsale, and Colonel Colthurst, with a view to establish a Fishery Board in Ireland, and to increase this loan, but it fell through. In conclusion I commend the fishing industry of Ireland to the earnest consideration of every well-wisher of the country.

The *Builder* went on to comment:

The above letter has brought forth another very practical and interesting letter from the Rev. T. Jasper Smyth, the Rector of Rathberry, county Cork, 'an owner of some small estates, and the most of whose labourers and tenants are fishermen.' "He furnishes some useful statistics, and gives an account of what has been done in the past, and what is required to be done at present, to promote the fishing industry. Mr. Smyth has proved himself to be a true friend of our fishermen, and his efforts to promote legislation in favour of this national industry are entitled to the thanks of all classes . ."

This introduces a remarkable story which reflects great credit on a handful of generous people and greater credit still on fishermen in County Cork who proved, for all time, that Irish fishermen, given the smallest encouragement, can operate as intelligently and effectively as any in the world.

As far back as 1863 Miss (later Baroness) Burdett-Coutts, daughter of Sir Francis Burdett, the celebrated English radical and friend of Ireland, assisted the fishermen of West Cork who had suffered through a potato failure. In 1879 she again came forward and through her financial aid a thriving fishery was set up. Father Davis, at her request, drew up a report of the conditions on Cape Clear island and, in consequence, she undertook to assist the Cape Clear and other islanders to obtain the appliances for carrying on mackerel fishing. The parish priest sent her the names of a number of the men whom he thought deserving of encouragment. The story of the rise of this industry was told in an article in the *Pall Mall Budget* by T. P. O'Connor, MP. The plan adopted was this: a boat with nets cost on an average £650; the intending owner or owners received from the Baroness from £250 to £300 and, in some cases, they added something from their own savings, and the remainder of the money was allowed by the builders to stand out — on no mortgage, be it remarked, further than the word of Father Davis. The term imposed by the Baroness was the repayment without interest of 10 per cent annually of the amount lent; thus, if the loan was £300 the annual repayment was £30 and the whole sum would be repaid in ten years. In some cases the rate of repayment was 5 per cent extending over twenty years. By October 1884 between £6,000 and £7,000 had been advanced in this way. Another part of the arrangement was that the Baroness, instead of taking up the principal, re-lent it and so always kept it in circulation among the fishermen. The fleet for 1885 numbered forty-four boats.

"The average earnings of these boats was some £500 each; thus the islanders earned £22,000 between them. The 'Capers' as the inhabitants of Cape Clear were called, in their short experience of four years became the most skilful, the most daring and the most successful of the fishermen of all nationalities coming to the fishing grounds. Whenever an English or a Scotch boat wished to say that a night had been particularly tempestuous, he remarked that the 'Capers did not go out'. The periodical victims of starvation were able to earn sometimes £100 in a lucky night; they had cheque books; houses with good slate roofs sprang up. Baltimore, a decaying village, became the centre of a great industry; in its small and beautiful harbour there floated during the season three or four hundred fishing boats. Lines of steamers conveyed the fish daily to Milford and thence to all the centres of population in England. Representatives of all the great fishing firms sent out boats every morning at nine o'clock when the report of the market prices had been received and eagerly competed for the purchase of the fish on the returning boats. Hundreds of labourers were employed at 25 s. a weeks and not a man in Baltimore or the surrounding district was idle during the whole season. The Fishing Board followed the example of the Baroness in making loans and several of the fishermen, besides punctually paying the instalments, invested their savings in new boats. Finally, the fishermen, without one exception, paid to the day and to the penny the amount advanced to them in loan." These were cheering results showing what might be accomplished through developing the fisheries of this country, through loans to fishermen and the provision of suitable piers and harbours for shelter and refuge.

In 1887 Baroness Burdett-Coutts opened at Baltimore the first Industrial Fishery School ever founded. It had been hoped that this could be started as a private venture, but to equip and run a building with classrooms, dormitories, recreation room, library, fishing gear, charts and other necessities was beyond the purse of the philanthropic

The Fishery School, Baltimore

The workroom in Baltimore Fishery School

baroness. Recourse therefore had to be made to the Industrial School Act to enable government funds to be tapped. This had the disadvantages that the boys recruited had to come from destitute families and be without visible means of subsistence, and must leave at the age of sixteen. Many youngsters who could have benefited from the excellent instruction provided were therefore excluded, and those let in (at ten years old as a rule) had to leave too soon. Nevertheless the school achieved notable success.

The school was run on very advanced lines — there were even women instructors. Four large fishing smacks were attached to the schools and older boys were in them all the time, two to each. These boats were employed in drift-net fishing for mackerel and herrings, trawling and long-line fishing. Several smaller boats were also attached and engaged in foreshore fishing manned almost wholly by students of twelve years and upwards. Four net machines were operated and nets were made not only for the school boats but for fishermen all along the West Cork coast. Local fishermen got their nets mended there. Boat building and cooperage were also carried on and there was instruction in fish curing.

In 1891, the year before he died, Father Davis wrote for the newly-constituted Congested Districts Board (which was at last to undertake long-needed improvements for the west coast fishermen) a pamphlet entitled 'Fishery Education'. He urged the establishment of a whole series of fishery schools to dissipate the ignorance in which the fishing population had so long been kept, and provided details of the successes of the Baltimore school, whose promoters had 'every reason to congratulate themselves on the results achieved in a very few years'. Fishery experts from Hull and Grimsby had been 'enthusiastic in their admiration'. Father Davis emphasised the general education given and noted that seamanship and navigation were taught as well as fishing expertise. He suggested the enlargement of the school, the acquisition of more boats, the introduction of small bursaries and the widening of the base from which recruitment took place. He also proposed the recruitment under indenture of boys over sixteen years of age discharged from ordinary Industrial Schools (detention centres).

Cover of the pamphlet The Harvest of the Sea for Ireland, *published to publicize the work of the Baltimore Fishery School in 1895*

Four years later in 1895 an English-man interested in the care of orphans, Henry S. Newman, visited the Baltimore School and wrote a pamphlet on it called 'The Harvest of the Sea for Ireland'. The number in attendance had risen from 100 to 150; gymnastics and field sports had been introduced; Newman saw fish-boxes being manufactured; the students were allowed a large degree of self-government; the recruitment base had been broaden-ed. Sir Thomas Brady, the Fisheries Inspector, already mentioned, had drawn attention to a nineteen year old, son of the school's fishery inspector, who after training at the school had become skipper of a first-class smack, worth with gear up to £700, and manned by a crew of seven. Some 40 per cent of those who had passed through the school were fishing or net-making (surely fewer than must have been hoped — most of the rest were in trade or farming). But more funds were required to increase the number of vessels attached to the school and to add to the accommodation. And indeed it was shortage of funds that prevented the auspicious dawn which the Baltimore school represented from brightening into daylight at last for our so long neglected fisheries. Nevertheless, Newman was able to write that after the baroness's initia-tive had formed the nucleus of a fishing fleet it had 'since expanded into a numerous fleet of first-class boats, second to none in the United Kingdom for skilled seamanship and efficiency'. A similar fishery school was opened at Killybegs but it lasted for a shorter period. The Baltimore school was still operative, in a low key, in the 1940s.

In October 1894 *The New Ireland Review* had printed 'A Plea for Arklow'. After discussing the vagaries of fish behaviour, including the recent tem-porary disappearance of the herring from the Arklow region, the author referred to the Irish fishermen's aptness to learn and readiness to make the most of the most meagre opportunities. He praised the Baltimore project and then went on to explain the way in which takings were shared out in Arklow fishing vessels. The owner, having supplied the boat itself, nets and chandlery, took half the receipts less the men's keep. The other half was divided among the crew in minutely adjusted proportions —

$$1\tfrac{1}{4}\ \tfrac{1}{8} : 1\tfrac{1}{8} : 1 : \tfrac{3}{4}\ \tfrac{1}{8} : \tfrac{3}{4} : \tfrac{1}{2}\ \tfrac{1}{8} : \tfrac{1}{2}$$

the first being the skipper's share and the last the boys. He thought the consistent absence of recriminations at Arklow over the application of so complicated a system spoke very highly for the Arklow fishermen.

Arklow fishermen had taken £7,000 worth of herring in one week in November 1876; cod and oysters were the only local fishing available but the Arklow men were venturing as far as Shetland to fish. (They had long been visiting West Cork for mackerel in season.) The average annual expenditure on nets by an Arklow fishing boat owner was over £4,000 and over £45,000 had recently been expended on improving Arklow harbour — proof that all the years of agitation for harbour improve-ment had at last had some effect. The article in *The New Ireland Review* estimated the number of Arklow fishing craft in 1894 at 160, of which 70 made up the mackerel fleet, and the total number of first- and second-class fishing vessels on the East coast at over 3,000, with well over that number classifiable as third-class. The author lamented that the owners of virtually all these craft had to purchase their nets outside Ireland and made a powerful case for the establishment of a net factory in Arklow.

The author of the article in *The New*

The harbour at Arklow. Fishing craft at the turn of the century

The Downings' Fishery, Co. Donegal, built up by the Congested Districts' Board at the end of the nineteenth century

Ireland Review met a retired fisherman in Arklow who had been living in destitution after the death by drowning of his son. He was now being cared for by the community of local fishermen — a wonderful case of the 'self-help' so dear to Chief Secretary Forster and *The Economist* but a sombre reflection on the type of society which their kind of thinking had produced. The young man, moreover, had been drowned after his lugger put to sea in defiance of a storm warning at the local coastguard station, because a period of poor fishing had left all the fishermen penniless and they could afford to stay ashore no longer. This kind of tragedy has occurred of course times out of number across the world to fishermen and is one of the arguments in favour of a basic minimum wage for fishermen.

The Congested Districts Board had been established, and in 1890 serious fishery research had at last been inaugurated on a large scale. The impressive volume issued in 1902 by the recently constituted Department of Agriculture and Technical Instruction under the title *Ireland Agricultural and Industrial* stated: 'Although Ireland can show a long and honourable record of work in the field of marine biology, it is only within comparatively recent years that the practical utility of such work in connection with the administration and development of our fisheries has received public recognition. The first step in this direction was the organisation in 1890 and 1891 by the Royal Dublin Society of a survey of the fishing grounds of the west coast.' The survey was carried out in chartered steam-yachts, the *Fingal* in 1890 and the *Harlequin* in 1891, with a Fisheries Inspector as director. The government contributed less than half the cost. *Ireland Industrial and Agricultural* remarks that before the survey the fisheries on the west coast were almost non-existent, and that in consequence of it a great development had since taken place.

In 1898 the RDS entered the field of fishery research again with an admirable project for establishing a marine laboratory to undertake a five-year study of mackerel and salmon. The laboratory was set up in February 1899 in a purchased 220 ton brigantine, the

Helga, No. 1. This 375-ton twin-screwed steamer was equipped both as a fishery protection vessel and as a fishery research ship. There has not been her equal since

FISHERIES-IRELAND.

52 & 53 Vic., c. 74, And any Acts incorporated therewith.

Trawling from Steam Vessels off part of the Coast of the County of WEXFORD.

BY-LAW.

We, the Inspectors of Irish Fisheries, in pursuance of the powers and authorities in us vested by the "Steam Trawling Ireland Act," (1889), do make and ordain the following By-Law, by which it is prohibited, and it is hereby prohibited to use from any Steamer or Steamship, or Vessel propelled by steam, the method of fishing known as Trawling, off that part of the Coast of the County of Wexford comprised within the space bounded by imaginary lines drawn from Crossfarnoge Point near Kilmore to the North Point of the Island called North Saltee—and from the Southern point of the said Island of North Saltee to the North point of the Island called South Saltee—and from the South point of the said Island of South Saltee to Coningmore Rock, and from said Coningmore Rock to Coningbeg Light Ship, and from said Coningbeg Light Ship to the Barrels Rock Light—and thence to Carnsore Point; said space within which such Trawling is hereby prohibited being marked blue on the map or plan annexed.

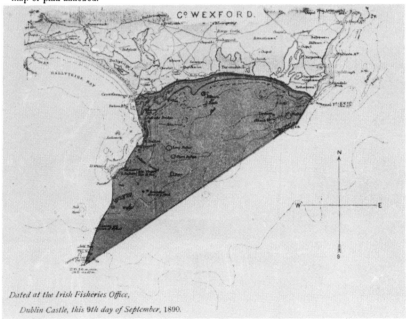

Dated at the Irish Fisheries Office,

Dublin Castle, this 9th day of September, 1890.

THOMAS F. BRADY,
ALAN HORNSBY,
WM. SPOTSWOOD GREEN, } *Inspectors of Irish Fisheries*

By the LORD LIEUTENANT and PRIVY COUNCIL in IRELAND.

ORDERED—That the said By-Law be, and the same is hereby approved.

Given at the Council Chamber Dublin Castle, the 28th day of January, 1891.

(P6) 250, 2, 91. Dublin: Printed FOR HER MAJESTY'S STATIONERY OFFICE, By ALEX. THOM & Co. (LTD.) 94, 95 & 96 Middle Abbey Street.

This proclamation is evidence of the start of fishing research and conservation in the last years of the nineteenth century after decades of pressure from various progressive interests

Saturn of Galway. Soon after, the Fisheries Branch of the new Department of Agriculture and Technical Instruction took over the laboratory and its four attendant boats, and the whole business of fishery research. This work was supplemented by the provision of a fishery protection cruiser, the first *Helga*, a fast twin-screw 345 ton steamer, 150' by 23' by 10'6", built at Ayr in 1891, very suitable for fishing herself and invaluable for preventing poaching and infringements of fishery regulations. She was originally a steam-yacht which the Department had had largely reconstructed. The second *Helga,* later L.E. *Muirchu,* was built for the Department in 1908 and was probably the fastest vessel of her type in service in these islands. Her two sets of triple-expansion engines could drive her in an emergency at 14½ knots, far faster than any trawler of the time. Her dimensions were 155' by 24'6" by 13'6" and she was specially fitted for fishery research work, her equipment including a fine laboratory. Moreover she was built in Ireland, by the Dublin Dockyard Company.

All these activities unquestionably led to an upsurge in our fisheries, even if it was the steam trawlers and drifters of Milford and other British ports which did the greater part of the fishing round Ireland. Already in 1902 the Department in its great book was warning that the steam fleets were 'prowling ceaselessly', and declaring that the fishing grounds were bearing the strain only 'fairly well'. 'How long can it last?' the book asked. In fact, the first application of serious research to our fisheries coincided with the first warnings that fish resources are not inexhaustible. The tension between research and exploitation, which lends such vivid drama to the fishery scene round Ireland today, had begun.

Ireland Industrial and Agricultural

has some splendid illustrations and descriptions of the fishing craft in use on our fishing grounds in 1902. A thoughtful official of the Department was at the same time arranging for the construction of models of each, foreseeing that the day of pulling and sailing fishing craft was rapidly closing. Many of these models can be seen at the National Maritime Museum in Dun Laoghaire. One of the book's illustrations is of a mackerel seine boat and 'follyer', another of a Kinsale mackerel boat riding to her nets. Also illustrated are an Arklow mackerel boat of 45 tons, a Skibbereen nickey of the same size, a 20 ton hooker and one of the big 70 foot French mackerel boats that were keeping up the old French traditions of fishing round Ireland.

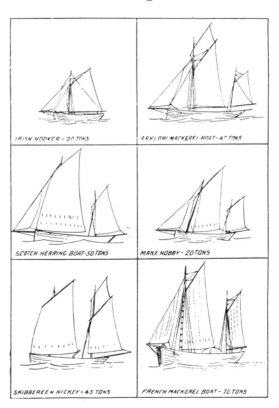

Different types of fishing boats seen around the British Isles in 1900. Taken from Ireland Industrial and Agricultural, *1902*

There are photos of an Arklow mackerel boat and of 'zulus' and 'nobbies' built in Connemara by local builders under the direction of a Department instructor. These pictures and the Museum's models recall nostalgically the magnificent struggle put up by the fishing industry of our country in the last days of sail and oar fishing, when the world was careering towards universal mechanisation, automation and war.

With the Department in overall control of the industry and responsible, within the limits set by government guidelines and current economic theory, for evolving an Irish fishery policy, with the Congested Districts Board empowered to give genuine help to the industry in the west, and with research being practically applied, Irish sea fisheries began to move towards a modest prosperity. Between 1905 and 1910 fish exports

from Ireland (including shellfish which decreased slightly) grew by some 50 per cent, from 22,574 tons to 33,927.

Seven experienced Arklow crews of deep-sea fishermen were brought by the Congested Districts Board to Galway bay, as well as nets, boxes and a cargo of ice, to help sceptical Aran islanders to develop a spring mackerel fishery. Instructors went to sea with them and, quite quickly, fishing in the area became profitable on a self-supporting basis. Similar methods stimulated fishing in other decayed fishing centres. A new mackerel fishery was opened in Blacksod bay at the turn of the century, adding considerably to the resources of the then very large and poverty-stricken local population. In 1901 the Donegal herring fishery was unprecedentedly successful, the fishermen earning £25,000 net, while persons engaged

Ardglass, 1900 showing steam trawlers, nobbies and nickeys

Herring curing at Ardglass. Note the herring girls in the right foreground

ashore in curing took in another £5,000. Conger, skate, cod, ling and glasson were profitably fished at Teelin and Aran. From 1886 to 1901 there was a lucrative export trade of mackerel to the United States and contemporary photos of Kinsale, Berehaven, Killybegs and other ports jammed with Irish mackerel boats testify to the rising tide of confidence on which the industry was floating. Pressure through the new Department had even got the British Foreign Office to seek markets for Irish fish, as can be seen from an analysis from the British Embassy in Madrid of possible outlets in Spain published in the *Department of Agriculture and Technical Instruction Journal* Vol II (1901–02) p. 496 ff.

In ten years the Congested Districts Board was responsible for getting ninety-one vessels worth £15,000 built in Ireland, twenty-three of them in depressed Donegal and Connemara. In the same years, in dazzling contrast with the record of the Board of Works in the whole half-century before, no less than £100,000 was spent on harbour improvements in the west alone.

Trawling had been practised in Ireland for 200 years. Otter trawls had come in in the 1860s. 40–70 ton beam trawlers were now operating out of Dublin, Dun Laoghaire, Galway and Dingle, and County Down ports were noteworthy for the larger size of otters in proportion to the size of the boats. Now in the first decade of the new century a few steam trawlers were acquired. There was a considerable mussel and a large periwinkle export. A very small prawn fishery also existed. Dunmore East

A mussel scraper or "arm iascáin" as it was known in Irish. Used for scraping mussels off the rocks it is now obselete. Made out of an old shovel, the blade was cut off short and provided with a straight edge. The shovel had a cylindrical socket into which the handle was fitted

researched. Of the years 1900—20 he wrote:

> The development of the inshore fisheries was an important part of the [Congested Districts] Board's responsibilities and much good work was undoubtedly accomplished. Boats and gear were provided by means of loans to approved applicants. . . the percentage of arrears and bad debts was relatively low. But the introduction. . . of the marine motor engine caused a revolution in the economics of the inshore fishing industry. Where a hard-working ambitious fisherman could have outfitted himself with a sailboat and gear for say £300, the sum needed jumped to £1,200 or £1,400 when he came to acquire a motor fishing boat. At the start, specially selected men had to be coaxed to make this change . . . and it was necessary to provide them with the services of instructors and also to subsidise them in other respects. Even with such encouragement there was, for a year or two, no great demand forthcoming for the motor boats, and little or no money was lost by the Exchequer on the foot of loan transactions. [He seems to mean that fraudulent Irish fishermen shunned the new method of propulsion, J. de C.I.] But the advent of war conditions in 1914 changed all that. The diversion of the British trawling fleets to war duty left open to our inshore fishermen the valuable English market.

was doing well on herrings and, as in the eighteenth century, Irish herrings had a very high reputation in the export markets. North Germany and the United States were steady buyers of our herrings. The annual income of Irish fisheries was reckoned in 1911 to be £400,000, worth perhaps about £5 million in today's money.

V.D. Rush of the Irish Sea Fisheries Board of those days wrote in the Maritime Institute's journal *Manannán* of July 1946 about our fisheries in the years between the start of this century and the foundation of the state. He was much more accurate on that period than on the earlier history of the industry, which he had evidently never seriously

Prices rose, the demand for motor boats soared, Britain faced serious food shortages and its government willingly lent Irish fishermen money to equip themselves to meet these. But, wrote Rush, 'many persons with an imperfect knowledge of the business took to sea fishing' and got powered

Building Coonanna pier, Cahirciveen, Co. Kerry and gutting fish in the foreground

Fishermen's cabins (early twentieth century)

craft on their own guarantee and that of hastily scrutinised sureties. With prices so high borrowers easily met the fixed half yearly instalments on their loans and still made a handsome living. No attempt was made by the offer of special discounts to induce them to repay more quickly, as they could have. 'A rude awakening', Rush went on, 'came by 1920 when the recommissioned British trawling fleet had resumed its landings of cheap and plentiful supplies of fish in all varieties. Our people found themselves heavily over-capitalised with boats and gear purchased at peak prices, but without outlets for their catches. The loans advanced during the period 1915—17 were by 1920—23 not half cleared, and many borrowers growing demoralised withdrew from the industry leaving their costly motor boats to rot at their moorings.'

By 1923 of course a separate Irish state had at last been founded. The Irish people and the Irish fishermen were entitled to expect the implementation, for the first time in history, of an Irish national fisheries policy based on consultation with fishermen themselves and fishery research workers, and worked out in the light of the true economic interests of the people as consumers and producers. They got nothing of the sort. Such a policy has not even yet been elaborated, though changing circumstances and the bitter experience of fifty years of frustration have at last made its elaboration as practical a possibility as it is an indispensable necessity.

In November 1911, after a careful study of the problem, Arthur Griffith wrote in *Sinn Féin*:

We dare say the number of public men in Ireland who realise that the sea fisheries of this country could be an industry second only to agriculture might be counted on one hand. We affirm that with a national government in this country the sea fisheries of Ireland and the other dependent industries could be made in ten years to yield three million pounds

Baiting night lines, Rathlin Island about the turn of the century

Ovoca, a model of the first motor trawler built in these islands, constructed at Tyrrell's Yard, Arklow, 1907. She continued to fish for more than fifty years

to the national wealth. We affirm that in the same period and under the same direction a hundred thousand people would find employment in connection with our sea fisheries, and four hundred thousand people would gain a comfortable livelihood through them.

Those words were written on the eve of the First World War. On the eve of the second the landings of fish were worth, in devalued pounds, less than half what they were in 1911 for all Ireland, and even if the Northern Ireland catch be added the figure still falls far short.

It is conceivable that, if Arthur Griffith had survived, the new state would not have forgotten its fishermen and the potential wealth of its fisheries. He was the one founding father of the new nation state who had clearly seen and bluntly said that our fisheries could be as great a source of wealth for us as our agriculture. This diligent little man, whose virulent anti-semitism and bitter suspicion of trade unionism would make him seem a strange and alien figure if still with us, whose masterpiece *The Resurrection of Hungary* bristles with faults and gapes with omissions, and whose dual monarchy theories were kicked rudely into the ebbing tide by the march of history, was nevertheless the architect of the economic theories on which, hesitatingly under Cosgrave and passionately under Lemass when Minister for Industry and Commerce, the economic foundations of modern Ireland were built. He did not easily let go of visions, even if impossible of realisation, and such a stubborn personality would surely not have allowed to disintegrate the realisable vision of an Ireland thriving from exploitation of its greatest neglected resource. He would not have been an easy task-master for the fishing community and he might not easily have sought or gained its confidence. But had he survived fishing would surely not have been allowed to slip back again from the crested years of hope to the trough of depression where it was to lie inert for so long. The surest legacy left to posterity by this most controversial figure was his conviction that we could and must build national prosperity on intelligent use of the wealth in the seas around us.

7

Ireland's Sea Fisheries during the First Forty Years of Independence

When the new state came into being our fishing fleet was very mixed, including a few steam trawlers, some steam drifters of up to 80 feet, motor vessels, a variety of sailing craft and a large number of rowing boats. It declined in size between the wars, changing somewhat in composition with the gradual disappearance of sailing craft, but was subject to no guiding policy. Above all, there was no drive to train fishermen, such as had begun in the last decades of direct British rule, and the resources in manpower and cash applied to oceanographic and specifically fishery research dwindled drastically.

At the end of 1922 a Minister for Fisheries was appointed, a step which appeared to herald serious attention being paid to the potentialities of our fisheries along the lines foreshadowed by Griffith. The Minister's function turned out, however, to be purely administrative; he was kept busy in 1923 amalgamating the two governmental bodies hitherto concerned with fisheries, the fishery branch of the Department of Agriculture and Technical Instruction and the fishery side of the Congested Districts Board, which was dissolved that summer. In June 1924 the Department of Fisheries emerged, charged also with the administration of rural industries, an early sign that the government of the day was not concerned to inaugurate a single-minded national campaign of fishery development. All the engineering staff save one individual employed by the Congested Districts Board in harbour construction and maintenance, and its dredging plant, were handed over to the Board of Works. This was ominous.

Soon came the downgrading of fisheries. For decades they were shuffled between the Departments of Lands and Agriculture as a minor appendage of one or the other; fisheries, so far as the country's rulers were concerned, had as their chief apparent function the provision of a parliamentary secretaryship, to be held for a short period by ambitious politicians serving their junior apprenticeship on the lowest rung of the hierarchical ladder. In September 1928 the Minister for Fisheries and his Department became the Minister and Department of Lands and Fisheries. In 1934 the functions of the Minister for Lands and Fisheries in respect of fisheries were transferred to the Minister for Agriculture, and in 1957 back to the Minister for Lands.

In 1929 vocational classes that the Congested Districts Board had run to give some very elementary fishery training were discontinued. The site used in Galway was handed to the Board of Works for disposal, and the marine motor shop there was also closed.

Fish curing, Clare Island (early twentieth century)

Subsidies hitherto paid to certain In-dustrial Schools for instruction in boat-building were dropped. Apprenticeships for coopering for boys from fish-curing areas (fish was exported in wooden barrels then) were introduced but very soon abolished, and as early as 1923 fish transit subsidies were terminated. Scientific research virtually ended, and the Fisheries Branch of the Department did not even have a laboratory until 1950.

Careful examination of the above list of measures would probably convince an impartial observer that for a period of about a quarter of a century the various governments that controlled the fate of the Irish people wished positively to kill the industry, the potential of which generation after generation had admitted and which had actually begun to prosper in the last period of British rule. This conclusion would be unfair, however. It was not hostility but ignorance and indifference that caused the governments of those days to neglect our fisheries and annul so many measures introduced under British administration to help them. Irish nationalism had turned its back on the sea and it has taken a very long struggle to reopen the eyes of the Irish people to the importance of the sea and to the greatness of its own mari-time traditions.

In the 1920s Irish sea fishermen concentrated on the fluctuating herring and mackerel shoals and only a small minority kept a tiny inshore fishery alive based on plaice, cod, haddock and whiting, and on the traditional shell-fisheries. Had these men had the backing of up-to-date research and had new entrants into the industry had full training, the foundations would have been laid of a fishing industry so pros-perous that today we would probably be able to play the leading role in

Kilkeel, c. 1925. N55, Mary Joseph, was the last of the nobbies

Steam trawlers at Killybegs

developing a Common Market fisheries policy. (It was foreign scientists like the Frenchman J. Le Gall who made nearly all the important discoveries about fish-behaviour off our coasts in these years, for instance that the time of appearance of herring on grounds fished by French steam trawlers off NNW Donegal at the edge of the deep water coincided with that of their disappearance from the area worked by drift-net fishermen. Conscientious Irish officials like G.P. Farran, Inspector of Fisheries, could do little more than tag along behind.)

In the first few years after the First World War the herring catch averaged about 5,500 tons, with Howth by far the most productive port followed by those of West Donegal. Between 1921 and 1923 the herring and mackerel catch, more than 60 per cent of the total, fell by nearly 56 per cent in quantity and over 50 per cent in value. In the later 1920s the annual average rose to some 10,000 tons, with North Donegal, Donegal bay, West Donegal and Waterford and East Cork in that order outstripping Howth. (Howth had fifty-two boats, all motor or steam, catching herring for three months in 1923, eighty-five in 1924 giving three months employment to 840 men at an average of £3 10s. 0d. a week.)

In the early 1930s, for a variety of reasons including the world depression, foreign competition and the fishermen's inevitable helplessness, given the absence of research support in the face of the erratic behaviour of herring shoals, the herring fishery virtually collapsed. In 1932 only some 2,000 tons were caught, with West Donegal ports in the lead followed by Wicklow and Wexford. Even in 1940 and 1941, when wartime conditions once more caused prices to rise, the catch averaged below 4,000 tons, less than in 1922 and only 12 per cent of the record 1911 herring

catch of 32,627 tons worth £166,544, as much incidentally as the value of the whole of this state's catch, all types of fish in 1938.

Along with the collapse of the German and Central European markets for cured herring in 1928–9 under stress of the world slump, there came also the collapse of the market in the United States for cured mackerel: our industry was in danger of virtual disappearance. Our own country was affected by the world crisis and its own internal and external problems and fish consumption at home was, per head, almost the lowest in Europe. There was no authority with the power to campaign, as Bord Iascaigh Mhara has been doing since 1962, for increased consumption at home, and fish had come home more and more to be looked on as a penitential dish, to be avoided except when virtually obligatory. Much of what was eaten at home was imported from Britain.

Then, at the time influential, *Catholic Bulletin* of May 1934 wrote of our fisheries being 'in a most lamentable plight', showing 'little or no sign of recovery, still less of progress'. It stated that 'our seas are despoiled by foreign craft, systematically, even recklessly', and had the wisdom, in this article signed 'Molua' (who was he?) to suggest that the nation badly needed a naval defence force, with vessels suitable for fishery protection, and a fish manure industry, and proper fishery research, including the use of aircraft to track shoals.

As early as 1925, recognising the precarious situation of the industry, a number of fishermen organised themselves into The Irish Fishermen's Association, open to 'all who are engaged in fishing for a livelihood in Irish inland or coastal waters', as well as to 'non-fishermen approved of by the local branch committee, and willing to subscribe

£1' per year. The Association's aims were to protect and forward the interests of fishermen; to unite fishermen into an organised body able to speak up on their behalf; to encourage and foster improved methods of catching and marketing fish; to cooperate with any body or person working for similar objectives. So, with P.J. Tuohy as general secretary and representatives from seven areas and under the rather improbably chairmanship of Colonel Maurice Moore and treasureship of Professor E.P. Culverwell, Professor of Education at TCD, this first of many associations was launched in the new state to try to organise a body of men who, though the guardians of a great tradition, had become disillusioned, suspicious and uncooperative. Success in this type of venture was still a long way off and those pioneers would no doubt be astonished and delighted at the distance which attempts at organisation have covered since their day, with the emergence of the Irish Fishermen's Organisation, the Salmon and Inshore Fishermen's Association and the Fisher-ies Branch of the ITGWU. All honour to them, and to later pioneers in this field, difficult and mistaken though they often showed themselves, such as Captain Segrave Daly and Seamus Rickard of Howth, of Muintir na Mara.

In 1927 the Irish Labour Party and Trade Union Congress issued a 3d. pamphlet *Labour and Ireland's Sea Fisheries*. It was largely the work of the party leader, Thomas Johnson, who had long worked in the mackerel export industry. It pays tribute to Darrell Figgis who had compiled for the first Dáil Éireann a 'Report on the Sea Fisheries', following the appointment by the Dáil, largely under Griffith's inspira-tion, of a sub-committee on sea fisheries to the Commission of Enquiry into The Resources and Industries of Ireland.

The pamphlet ran to some 10,000 words. It started from the principle that the fishing industry is a social service, operating in a situation of permanent uncertainty in the national interest. It went on to propose the creation of a national fishing fleet composed of the vessels of a series of local co-operative

Fish gutting at Killybegs

organisations, each represented on a national fishery council, which would be both the advisory body for the Minister for Fisheries and his organ for administering fishery policy. This had to include thorough exploitation of the fishery resources in Irish waters, protection of the livelihood of the individual fisherman and the maximum possible development of scientific fishery research in support of the industry. The industry would be entirely self-supporting through the catching and marketing activities of the cooperative societies, which would become profit-making concerns for the benefit of their members. The state's only financial liability would be to pay for the research.

Of course none of the proposals in Tom Johnson's pamphlet was implemented — the Irish Fishermen's Association failed to organise the majority of the fishermen and eventually faded out; 'Molua's' suggestions about fish-manure factories and a naval service also got no hearing. The numbers engaged in fishing steadily declined: there were still 1,815 full-time fishermen in 1936 and 5,920 'occasionals', but two years later these figures had dropped to 1,463 and 5,888. Even high wartime prices only raised the number of full-timers to 1,925 in 1944 and 1,886 in 1945, though the number of 'occasionals' had gone up to 8,191 in 1945.

The industry was, in fact, in crisis, throughout the period between the wars and for years after the Second World War. Many fishermen were in debt for vessels which were becoming in many cases obsolete, and the boats were generally equipped with gear unsuited for making the catches of demersal fish necessary now that the herring and mackerel markets had vanished. There were, as there have always been, enlightened spirits who tried to awaken public opinion and the rulers of the nation to the understanding of the possibilities of the industry; but only one serious official action was taken to deal with the crisis. Inadequate though it was, it created a structure out of which was to emerge many years later the organisation upon which the future of the industry depends today: in November 1930 the Irish Sea Fisheries Association was set up by W.T. Cosgrave's last government.

Apart from the obsolescent steam trawlers of the Dublin Trawling, Ice and Cold Storage Co Ltd, for instance the 120 foot long and 223 ton *Father O'Flynn* built in 1906 and a few more (nine in all), the great majority of the country's fishing craft over 15 tons had been bought by individuals on wartime loans which had in many cases not been settled and in the prevailing conditions never would be. Arrears of repayments had amounted to only 6 per cent in 1918 but were as high as 60 per cent in 1926, and the provision of loans thereafter had been virtually halted by our new independent state. An inter-departmental committee of 1929–30 came to the conclusion that loans amounting to £100,000, a very large sum then, were irrecoverable, as might have been foreseen given the lack of any national fishery policy, any serious fishery research, any training scheme for fishermen and any system of certificates of competence for skippers. Incidentally, farmers were treated differently from fishermen a few years later: they are much more numerous and their electoral muscle has to be taken into account. They were granted as a 'patriotic' gesture to their patriotism remission of half their hire purchase payments on their land and the other half was assigned for improvement of their industry. It was evidently more honourable to be a small peasant landowner than a fisherman small fishing boat owner.

The idea after 1930 was to encourage skipper-owners to build up a new fleet through a hire-purchase scheme. Quite a large number of vessels, mostly between 30 and 40 feet long, with names beginning *Naomh* or *Pride of* and mostly built in Meevagh, Baltimore, Arklow and Killybegs was acquired, in the period 1931–8 by the Sea Fisheries Association of Saorstat Eireann Ltd. It set about the somewhat painful process of inducing fishermen to hire-purchase these.

In 1936 the Irish fishing fleet consisted of ninety vessels of 15 tons (net) and upwards, in all 2,528 tons, and 1,561 craft of under 15 tons. All had to be registered and marked with their port of registry by an Order of 17 December, 1927. By 1938 the number had shrunk to eighty-one vessels over 15 tons, 2,703 tons in all, and 1,409 vessels under 15 tons. The port with the largest registration of fishing vessels over 15 tons was Dublin; of these the newest was the steam trawler *Fort Rannoch* (113 tons net) built at Aberdeen in 1936 and owned by John Lewis of Aberdeen. She was taken over by the newly formed Irish navy, then called the Marine Service, and armed as a warship when the Second World War began. The next newest was a vessel built in Baltimore in 1920 and the rest were all pre-1914. The oldest, the *O'Neill*, had been built in Arklow in 1877 and was still owned there; originally a sailing vessel — there were still more than fifty of these fishing in 1938 — she had been fitted with a motor engine. Skibbereen was the port with the next largest number of registered fishing craft over 15 tons — fifteen in all, the newest built in 1921, the oldest in 1875. One, *Trimardeur,* was a sailing ship. (The Dublin fishing register carried five of these.)

This, then, was the fishing fleet with which we entered the Second World War. There was no overall government fishing policy and the Sea Fisheries Association, even had it wished to initiate one, had no power to do so. Nevertheless, the catch, little more than 10,000 tons valued at about £150,000 in 1936, was up to about 11,000 tons valued at £167,000 in 1938, to a value of £233,000 in 1939 and to some 23,000 tons valued at £680,246 in 1945. The increase may partly be credited to the efforts of the Sea Fisheries Association but more considerably to wartime demand. Already in 1946, the first year of peace, the catch's value had slumped to £434,000 and to 1947 to £374,193, little more than was produced by the much smaller Northern Ireland fleet in a much more limited area (£320,415). By 1947, incidentally, we had only three steam trawlers fishing against the nine before the war.

V.D. Rush of the Sea Fisheries Association summed up the industry's wartime achievement in an article in the Maritime Institute's journal *Mannanán* of July 1946 in these words: 'Our people are willing and anxious to increase production so long as there is a reasonable prospect of securing a fair return for their labours. The attainment of such conditions save as a temporary consequence of two world wars, has, unfortunately, not proved feasible in our times; but this should not be so.' In other words, we still had good fishermen who had been able to double production with only a minute increase in their full-time numbers, but we still had no national will to turn our long-known fishery potential into a reality of riches.

(It is appropriate here to mention that during the Second World War two Irish fishing vessels were lost by belligerent action; the Dublin Trawling, Ice and Cold Storage Co's 216 ton steam trawler, *Leukos*, built in Aberdeen in 1914, presumed lost with all hands, James

A steam trawler similar to the 'Leukos', the Dublin trawler lost with all hands in 1940, a war casualty, and the 'Father O'Flynn', the last of the Dublin steam trawlers

Thomeson, skipper; W. Donnelly, mate; A. McLeod and B. Smyth, engineers; P. McCarthy, cook; P. O'Scanlon, bosun; M. Cullen, fireman; J. Hawkins and J. Sumner, apprentices; T. Mulligan and A. Pill, deckhands, on 12 March 1940; and the Sea Fishery Association's *Naomh Garbhan*, sank by striking a mine on 2 May, 1945 losing John Griffin Jnr., skipper; John Griffin Snr. and N. Cuddihy, fisherman.)

Of the Association, which Rush called a 'benevolent autocracy', Colonel A.T. Lawlor, founder of the Maritime Institute of Ireland, wrote in 1945 in his *Irish Maritime Survey* that:

[It] 'was set up by the Government in 1930. Being dependent for their livelihood on the vagaries of weather and seasons, Irish fishermen in the past had very little opportunity of putting by any savings, and, as a consequence, were seldom in a position to provide, out of their own resources, the boats and gear necessary to win any sort of a decent livelihood from their hazardous calling.

For about fifty years prior to 1930, loans had been made to the fishermen out of certain funds, which, though of charitable origin, were administered through government agency. The loans granted were generally of small amounts, but from about 1910, when motor engines were being adopted in increasing numbers. . . the advances made to individual fishermen increased considerably. Accordingly, at the outbreak of war, in 1914, a modern, well-equipped fleet of small craft was in being, and our fishermen were in a position to reap the full benefit of the high prices obtainable.

They were able to repay promptly the half-yearly instalments on their loans and were, generally, quite well off . . . .

Then came the slump of 1921 from which the Irish fisheries . . . suffered, and from which they had not yet recovered by 1930. While the competent fishermen worked hard and carried on, the less experienced men lost heart and abandoned their boats. As many of the boats abandoned, as well as many of those kept in service, had been constructed at war-time prices, the position of those fishermen whose debts had not been extinguished or considerably reduced before the post-war slump, become acute, now became impossible, and a large proportion of the loans had to be written down in relation to the reduced value and earning power of the boats, with consequential heavy loss to the State.

The loan system, as previously worked, having thus proved a failure in the changed conditions, it was necessary to substitute something for it, if our fishermen were to be provided with the means of making their living. Accordingly, the Government of the day decided to set up a Co-Operative Association of Fishermen, with financial assistance from the State, which would provide selected members with boats and gear, the cost of the outfits to be repaid out of the sale price of catches. This was the origin of the Irish Sea Fisheries Association, Limited.

The main functions of the Association are thus the development of the sea-fishing industry by the provision of boats, engines and gear for members on hire-purchase terms and the co-operative marketing of members' catches.

The affairs of the Association are in the control of a Committee of Management comprising eight directors — four elected every three years by the members, and four (including the Chairman), nominated by the Minister of Agriculture — together with a Manager who is appointed by the Directors on the nomination of the Minister. The Directors do not receive any fees for their services. Funds are provided annually under the Vote for Fisheries. They consist of free grants to cover the cost of administration and for general development work, and also of advances which are repayable to the Exchequer for the purchase of boats and gear for issue to members on hire-purchase terms. Members to whom boats, engines or gear are issued on hire-purchase must make. . . a cash prepayment representing at least 20 per cent of the cost of the chattels. The normal arrangement in regard to repayment is that members pass to the Association each week an agreed proportion (usually 25 per cent) of their earnings after allowing for running expenses.... In this way the hire-purchaser is saved the anxiety of meeting demands for fixed half-yearly instalments during, perhaps, unsuccessful fishing seasons, as happened under the former loan system. When seasons are good, the members' repayments are comparatively high, while in slack times they are correspondingly low. . . . Currachs or small items of gear are supplied to part-time fishermen, on the basis of repayment by small, but fixed quarterly payments . . . .

It is a matter for congratulation that, during the last few years, over fifty fishermen-members have been enabled. . . to become the sole owners of valuable and well-equipped fishing vessels. In all, about one hundred and

Clogherhead, 1936. The motor fishing vessel was by now slowly ousting all other types

forty motor fishing vessels of various sizes have been issued. . . on hire purchase terms.

Colonel Lawlor went on to describe how every member of the Association had to enter into a marketing contract with it, and how the Association marketed the catches (in fact it handled little more than 20 per cent of the catch in 1945, 24 per cent the year before). He also pointed out that it maintained a boat-yard and engine shops and a mussel purification plant in Kerry to support the considerable mussel export trade. (Membership cost 6 s. on entry and 1 s. yearly for fifteen years thereafter).

This was very different from the kind of organisation visualised by Darrel Figgis and Tom Johnson, and as V.D. Rush said, its structure was autocratic

and offered the ordinary fisherman even less say in the direction of his industry than its constitution seemed to promise. Training and research were outside its scope, and its establishment had begun the curious dual control of fishing — Department-Association — with which the fishing industry still has to live. However, it was something, and the question after the end of the Second World War was whether it or any other agency would be able to prevent the still only convalescent industry from collapsing again into the morbid torpor from which it suffered after the First World War.

This time, however, conditions were different. In the first place the fisher-men themselves had learned from the vicissitudes of their industry in the past quarter-century. Secondly, there now

Landing fish, Co. Louth

existed the Sea Fisheries Association, with all its defects. Thirdly, Europe after the Second World War was very different from the Europe of the 1920s: ordinary people were determined to reward themselves for the suffering of the war years by raising their living standards — their earnings and their consumption, including consumption of fish. Fourthly, an era of new techniques was opening which was destined to make profound changes in the fishing industry. Finally, the Irish people was at length starting to awaken to the importance of the sea for the national future.

This awakening of the Irish people was most sharply reflected in the activities of the Maritime Institute of Ireland, founded in 1941 to fight for the imple-

mentation of a national policy for the development of a strong maritime economy and to revive national interest in Ireland's past maritime traditions. Colonel Lawlor's *Irish Maritime Survey* was essentially a statement of these aims to the public, the first influential call for an Irish maritime policy since Griffith more than thirty years before.

From the moment of its foundation the Institute was concerned with the future of Irish fisheries. From the start it saw that a coherent national fishery policy was required, and from the start it challenged the accepted idea that the Irish fishing industry could only be a small, small-boat, inshore industry. In September 1942 *The Maritime Magazine*, which was the Institute's organ during most of the years which the magazine lasted, printed an unsigned article entitled 'Our Fishing Industry'. This was a generally optimistic survey of the situation of the industry in that year. In September 1943 the same journal published an article, 'Modern Irish fishing vessels', by Jack Tyrrell of Arklow, one of the Institute's founders, in which he foretold far-reaching changes in the design of fishing craft and techniques of fishing. In December 1944 *The Maritime Magazine* printed an analysis of the annual report for 1943 of the Fisheries Branch of the Department, emphasising the importance of the few research projects — oyster breeding, examination of herring — which the Department was then able or financially permitted to carry out. In March 1945 the magazine reprinted an article from *The Irish Times* by 'An Aran Islander', calling for the creation of a national fishing fleet of fast ocean-going trawlers, backed by a proper training scheme and 'a marine zoology and research section. . . based on such fine work as that of the marine department of advanced Japanese research'. The Institute published Rush's article, based on a lecture he had given to Institute members, the following year in its own new journal *Mannanán*, and Captain D. P. Fortune, later for a time the Institute's honorary secretary, produced for it a 'Memorandum on fishery harbours' based on the correct calculation that fishing vessels were going to get bigger.

The Maritime Institute gave evidence before the post-war Commission on Vocational Education urging the development of fishery training schemes for Irish youths. It also urged that fishermen should be allowed into the national health insurance scheme.   In 1949

Greasing the sail of a pookawn, Aran Islands. The pookawn, much used for fishing, was the smallest vessel of the hooker type

Fishing from the cliffs, Aran Islands

the Institute gave detailed evidence before the Commission on Population and Emigration, compiled over many weeks by a sub-committee of which this writer was the convener. The Institute believes that its advocacy therein of sea-fish farming was the first time that the possibilities of aquaculture along our coasts were seriously put forward in public in Ireland. The Institute's evidence before the 1949 Commission included (1) a calculation that ultimately the Irish fisheries would be able to afford employment, afloat and ashore, to nearly as many as the 100,000 people visualised by Griffith, (2) a strong suggestion that there ought to be a separate Department of Fisheries with its own Minister and Parliamentary Secretary, (3) the development of a fishing fleet capable of operating not only inshore but above all in intermediate waters and even in distant water, (4) use of naval service vessels to help locate fish shoals and do other

research, (5) more adequate protection of fishing grounds from foreign poachers, (6) stimulation of the establishment of locally-based, self-governing fishery co-operatives, loosely associated but 'with the maximum of freedom from rigid state control' (the Sea Fisheries Association was considered too weak to be able to launch such a scheme), (7) official recognition of Muintir na Mara, the organisation which was then most representative of Irish sea fishermen, (8) an elaborate set of proposals for financing fishery progress, among them the creation of a special bank like the Danish Fiskeri Bank and a special levy of 1d. to 4d. in the pound on the rates in the maritime counties (county agricultural committees, it was noted, were spending the equivalent of a 1d. rate raised in the maritime counties on the important but surely less nationally urgent business of encouraging gardening and bee-keeping), (9) stimulation of exports to well above the £200,000 figure achieved in 1945, (10) the establishment of fish processing factories and (11) various steps to increase the consumption of fish at home.

The point was made by the Institute in its evidence that the annual cost of administration of the Sea Fisheries Association was little more than £12,000, 'the staff consisting of 33 persons, of whom only 5 are on the technical side at very small salaries, the Inspector of Fisheries being paid £409 p.a. and the Fishery Officer £300 p.a., the positions of Assistant Engineer and Technical Assistant being vacant'. And to rub in the shamefully neglectful attitude of government towards sea fishing it was emphasised that the net state aid to sea fisheries through the Association was £5,735 in 1945, when £160 was allotted by the Department from its vote under heading 'Scientific

Taking fish from nets, Aran Islands

Investigations, etc'.

With regard to Northern Ireland, the Institute made the following points:

Northern Ireland

"The value of fish landings in the Six Counties has been rising steadily for some years; in 1947 it was £320,415, almost as much as in the 26 counties, and 80% more than in 1941.

About 1936 Scottish boats began to fish off the coast of Co. Down, operating from Ardglass Harbour, and the success of their activities soon began to show the local men how they could profit by the example of the visitors. The Scottish vessels were new, and were equipped with modern powerful and economical diesel engines, variable speed winches, and such refinements as electric lighting, power driven hoses for washing etc. Their chief advance, however, was in the development of the seine net to a higher degree of efficiency than had previously been achieved, and this was made possible mainly by the new machinery for handling the fishing gear. The Scottish fishermen had found seine net fishing so profitable that several of their boats were fitted and equipped solely for this work. (Those adapted also for drift net fishing, were so occupied for only about 3 months of each year).

The Irish fishermen were not slow

in following the example given them. As a beginning, they installed new and more powerful engines in their boats, often with the assistance of Government loans, but in some cases the more thrifty were able to pay for all improvement without assistance. The new departure was successsful from the beginning, mainly due to the much smaller cost of the seine equipment and to the greater area which can be fished by it than by the older trawling or anchor-seining methods, coupled with the shorter time in which a 'shot' can be completed with the modern machinery.

The younger men were soon attracted by the possibilities of new fishing methods, and stayed on, taking a very active interest in their development. It was very soon seen by them that the fullest advantages could be taken and the greatest progress made only if they had modern vessels, particularly suited to their locality and to their tidal harbours. In this connection, the new vessels must have less draught than previously in order to be able to enter and leave the port at almost any state of the tide.

The Northern Government gave assistance in approved cases for new boats, and as many as were sound enough were reconditioned and modernised; the building up of the fleet continues, and at present it is estimated that there are about 40 boats each in Kilkeel and Portavogie, of from 10 to 25 nett registered tons capable of operating the seine fishing net efficiency. Each boat has a crew of 6 to 8 men, and new boats are being added as quickly as machinery and materials can be obtained. The most popular type of new boat is 50 feet long, 16 nett and 27 gross registered tonnage, with an 80 H.P.

Diesel engine, and a 3 speed winch with automatic rope coilers. Such a vessel costs about £5,000 and the fishing gear about £300. It should be added that these details refer to vessels primarily engaged at seine net fishing. There are of course a number of smaller craft which follow the older type of drift net fishing.

In the past few years returns have been exceptionally good; in conversation with many of the men engaged, they have expressed the view that, while war prices have been of some help prices are not greatly in excess of peace time levels, and that it is chiefly due to the greater catching power of their boats and gear that their success can be attributed. To improve matters still further the N. Ireland Government has since the war taken active steps to improve all Northern fishing ports.

From the point of view of the Commission on Emigration and Population, the most interesting aspect of Northern Ireland fishery development is in the large number of young men who have been attracted to the industry, and particularly that most of the owners of the newest boats are young men, in some cases only 24 years old. Those men are very keen on the adoption of new ideas and are not content with the 'rule-of-thumb' methods of their fathers. They are ready to accept any sound new idea in boats or machinery, and are constantly experimenting to improve their fishing gear.

It should be stressed that in fishing a very long apprenticeship is not required, and a healthy youth can expect to earn a 'man's share' in a short time after commencing. His progress to part or complete ownership in a boat depends on his own ability and energy, but even as a member of the crew, his earnings are good, and working conditions are by no means severe.

There is no question but that the recent development in N. Ireland, briefly outlined above, can equally well be adapted here. It is a fact that our fishermen are well aware of what is being done and are anxious to adopt the new methods, and it may be said that a step in this direction has already been made by a company operating at Howth. The great obstacle to development at the present time is that the materials and machinery for the building of suitable boats, and the necessary fishing gear, cannot be obtained during the emergency, but there is no question that Govern-

ment assistance could very profitably be given as soon as supplies are available to enable our own men to follow the example of their Northern neighbours.''

The fact was that, henceforth, whatever government was in power was going to be faced, if it started to let the fishing industry decline into its pre-war misery, with the determination and growing articulateness of the fishermen themselves and with slowly-awakening public conviction that the fisheries had a big future — guided chiefly by the Maritime Institute in a long series of public statements, letters to the press, newspaper articles, broadcasts and memoranda drawn up to keep official interest awake.

The 1950s were not famous for speedy

First new post-war trawler to come into Dun Laoghaire Harbour, 1955. Skipper Paddy Shortall

growth of the national and individual incomes. They were a period of massive emigration. Yet the fishing industry began its long slow upward move. Exports fell in 1950 to £144,000 from the £200,000 in 1945 but by 1959 they had increased in value sevenfold to £1,041,000. Consumption at home had doubled, from £386,000 worth to £773,000.

In 1950 the number of full-time fishermen had risen from the 1945 figure of 1,886 to 1,913 and £442,309 worth of fish was landed. The *Sunday Press* in a feature article on 23 September, 1951 called the industry 'moribund', claimed that we should have had 50,000 full-time fishermen and made a series of disparaging comparisons between our industry and Norway's, emphasising particularly that we had only four deep-sea fishing vessels, while of the 1,349 'other boats excluding rowboats', 730 were 'outmoded sailing vessels, and the balance of 619 motor vessels refers largely to very small boats confined to inshore fishing'.

In 1952 a number of important events occurred. The twenty-one year old Sea Fisheries Association was wound up as the state body charged with assisting the growth of the industry and An Bord Iascaigh Mhara (BIM) was established by a new Fisheries Act. It was a potentially more flexible organisation, carrying on not only the Association's functions of hire-purchasing vessels to would-be owners and marketing the catches of hire-purchasers, but also acting as the promotional authority for the industry. This proved to be a vital stepping stone in the industry's progress towards maturity, but in 1952 it was still only a stepping stone in a stream of swirling problems, a very long way from dry land.

As Arthur Reynolds of *The Irish Skipper* expressed it in a memorandum on BIM to the Maritime Institute a few

years later: 'BIM, while given a free hand on promotional matters in the fishing industry, does not have the powers to lay the foundations for sound promotion'. The memorandum showed that BIM ought to have been given authority to initiate research 'to ascertain for sure that there were fish available to support the intensified catching power' it was providing. Instead, the Fisheries Division of the Department of Agriculture and Fisheries remained the chief research body, 'orientated to churning out papers for international conferences where other nations can profitably utilise the findings of our costly, almost strictly long-term research'. The memorandum threw light on other restrictions on BIM's promotional activities: (1) fishery protection was the responsibility of the Department of Defence which would not, of course, take orders from BIM about where to send its corvettes to chase foreign poachers, (2) the price of fish was a matter for the Department of Industry and Commerce and unless it acted, BIM's efforts to lessen the too wide gap between what the fisherman received and what the housewife paid for fish would be frustrated, (3) trawlers needed the best, and frequently tested, life-saving gear, but to see they had it was the function of another section of an altogether different department (Transport) which is notoriously short of inspectors and (4) certain fishery harbours, badly needing improvement if BIM's promotional plans were to be fully effective, were the responsibility of the Board of Works, in its turn a direct responsibility of the Department of Finance which in the end was and is the body that could make or break fishery development by granting or with-holding money. BIM, the memorandum ended, should be given control of fishery research and of training of fishermen, and within it there should be — rather as Figgis and Johnson had long ago proposed, and the Institute in 1949 — a committee made up of persons from every sector of the industry, elected and not politically appointed, to advise. Finally, there would have to be a separate Department of Fisheries to supervise the implementation by BIM of a genuine promotional policy along these lines. The existence of the new body, therefore, was a stepping stone, but unless the new body could be moved forward in the right direction, the industry would still be left floundering.

Two other events in 1952 helped BIM to get moving. One was the in-auguration in the autumn of a new concrete pier at Killybegs, promised by all the various governments since 1931 when the wooden pier provided by the Congested Districts Board in 1897 began to give trouble. This was the first step towards Killybegs becoming the thriving fishing port which it now is. The second was the Order made in December removing the control which had kept fish prices unchanged since 1944; decontrol had been recommended by the Prices Advisory Board.

The Prices Advisory Board stressed the importance of the formation of BIM and stated that its policy was to increase home landings of fish, while at the same time promoting consumer

Killybegs, 1952. The old town pier

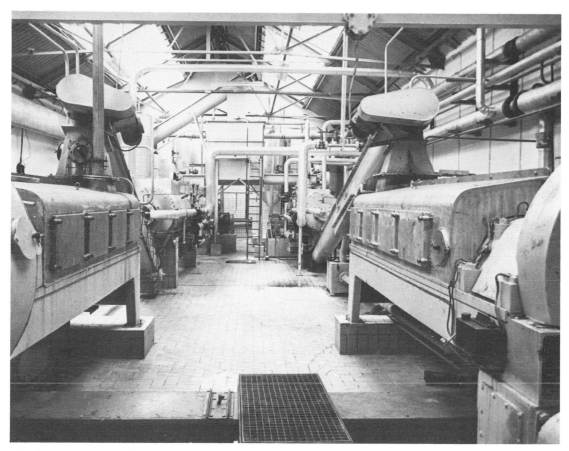

The fish meal and cold storage plant at Killybegs

demand. To further these ends the nucleus of an off-shore fleet had been acquired and arrangements had been made for the expansion of the whole-sale side of BIM's business. The Prices Advisory Board regarded this as important for, in its view, the present wholesale channels of distribution were far too narrow. The considered view of BIM was that the withdrawal of the control of fish prices and profit margins was desirable. Following on such withdrawal there might be, as there were in Great Britain, fluctuations in fish prices, but it was anticipated by BIM that the position would soon adjust itself. Finally, the report stated:

The Prices Advisory Body is of the opinion that the improvement of conditions in the industry to make possible the provision of adequate supplies of fresh fish at satisfactory prices cannot be achieved by price control applied to existing conditions, but must be dealt with on a much wider basis. Having regard to the evidence the Prices Advisory Board has recommended the removal of control over the prices of sea fish subject to the proviso that the position be reviewed after twelve months.

Prices in the event changed very little

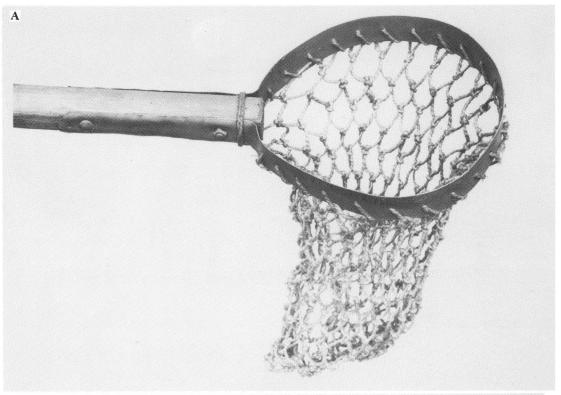

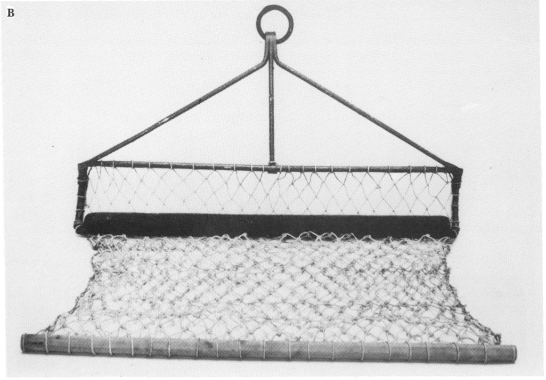

A *A "brídeog" used for dredging oysters in comparatively shallow water. It consists of a bag-shaped net mounted on a metal ring and carried at the end of a stout pole. The pole is about 3 m in length, the ring holding the net about 4 cm wide and 25 cm in diameter. The net is knitted of stout string and is about 40 cm long with a mesh of 3 cm side*

B *This oyster dredge, known as a 'billy dredge' consists of a rectangular iron frame forming the mouth of the net. The lower edge of this is in the form of a blade for scraping oysters off the bottom. This frame is 93 cm wide. The side pieces are concave and 16 cm high. The blade is 8 cm wide and its lower edge is provided with holes for attachment of the net. The upper part of the frame is provided with a triangular attachment for the towing line. This consists of two sloping side bars 50 cm long. The ends of these are twisted around the concave side members of the frame. The ring attachment is 9 cm in diameter. The net is about 90 cm wide and 65 cm long*

C *A scallop lifter made from a stout shaft, attached to a strong metal ring supporting the net bag*

D *A scallop dredge consisting of a triangular iron frame 110 cm high and 90 cm across at the base. There is a horizontal bracing bar, slightly convex in shape 75 cm from the apex. A thinner horizontal bar is also fixed 9 cm below. It too is convex and the upper edge of the net is fixed eleven large teeth each 6 cm long. Along the back edge of the bar, one between each pair of teeth is a series of ten holes through which the strands of the lower net edge are threaded. The mouth of the net is 25 cm deep; it is 75 cm long and its back edge is spread by a stout stick 100 cm long. The dredge is used for fishing scallops in eight to twelve fathoms of water. It is dropped into the sea mouth downwards and drawn along the bottom for 20 to 500 metres* in the next few months.

In December 1953 BIM issued its first annual report. It referred to quick-freezing, cold storage and fish meal pilot plants at Killybegs, to the prospects of developing fish meal production, and to three German fishing cutters recently brought into operation which had already caught 76 tons of fish sold for £10,070. They could operate beyond the inshore range and help to reduce the import of fish from abroad, an anomaly that had long been one of the salient features of the Irish fish markets, for instance £162,000 worth of fish and fish products imported in 1939, almost exactly the value of the fish landed by our own fleet. At the end of 1953 BIM had seventy-one boats out on hire-purchase, worth £200,000. That year saw more fish landed than any year since 1950 and for a greater value than any year since 1949.

1953 also saw the opening of a series of polemics, generally constructive in tone, in *Irish Fishing*, organ of An Comhlachas Iascaigh Mhara (the members of the former official Sea Fisheries Association who had held together) and edited by Seán de Cleir. This was the only journal concerned with the problems of the industry before the foundation, some time after the demise of *Irish Fishing*, of *The Irish Skipper*. It continuously urged that BIM should make the establishment of guaranteed fair prices for fish as landed its primary duty. It also printed interesting articles on scientific developments and research and on the problems of seasonal fluctuations in catches and price falls following sudden gluts, the fisherman's eternal headaches.

In 1954 landings by Irish fishermen satisfied the home market almost entirely, leading to a sharp fall in imports; 12,736 tons of fish were landed, some 16 per cent more than the previous year and worth about 15 per cent more. In Northern Ireland 6,700 tons were landed, 1,050 tons more than in 1953 and 1,350 more than in 1952, worth 13 per cent more than in 1953. Eight more fishing vessels over 25 tons operated in the Republic in 1954 than in 1953 and there was a drop in the number of smaller craft engaged — pointers to new tendencies growing up in the industry. Lobsters were being sold in Dublin at 4s. a pound, a phenomenon never likely to be seen again, since higher earnings have since then been a factor in a powerful rise in prices though, throughout the developed world, more products, such as lobsters, have come within the reach of a greater proportion of the population than ever before. Shellfish landings were growing year by year. In 1954 the naval service detained eleven trawlers for infringing our fishery limits.

In 1955 the quantity of fish landed rose by 19.2 per cent and in value by 7.9 per cent compared with 1954. Only two poaching foreign trawlers were detained by the corvettes of which our navy then consisted. The herring catch was up 41 per cent on the previous year. BIM continued to operate its own three trawlers, which landed rather more than 4 per cent of the total catch of demersal fish. Shellfish landings were up by 28 per cent in value compared with 1954. There was an increase of twenty-four in the number of vessels of over 15 tons fishing, but a sad decrease of ninety-five in the number of full-time and of 1,622 in the number of part-time fishermen.

As in several previous years there were no fatal accidents to fishermen, as there had been, for instance, in 1947 when two lobster fishermen were lost after their boat capsized off Dunmore East and three line fishermen from Killary harbour perished when their boat was driven on the rocks — reminders, that occur too frequently even today, of the fathomless treachery of the sea and the need for every fisherman to be trained and equipped to deal with it. The *Ros Eo* of Skerries, however, had a narrow escape on 21 March, 1947 when she struck the Cross Rock, which had been unmarked for months, while returning laden with over fifty boxes of fish. She survived only thanks to prompt assistance from another Skerries boat, the *Ros Mor*.

The 1955 Food and Agricultural Organisation Year Book announced that the total world catch of fish in 1953 had been 27 million metric tons, 20 per cent higher than in 1938. It was to double and more in the next two decades, a sobering reminder that, for all the steady increase in our own landings at 15,126 tons, on the edge of some of the world's finest fishing grounds, we still had a vast distance to travel to create the size and quality of fishing industry appropriate to our geographic situation.

1955 also saw completed the modernisation of Portavogie, County Down, as

The Arctic Swan, 52 feet, of a similar type to those built at Crosshaven in the mid 1950s

a fishing port at a cost of £250,000 — the cost sounded very high at the time but proved to be an excellent investment. In November 1955 BIM entered into a contract with a private boatyard at Crosshaven, County Cork for construction of two 56' 6" trawlers to be built in eight months of native oak and larch. Such additions to our fishing fleet less than a quarter of a century ago seemed to verge on the revolutionary. In 1955, moreover, the Dublin 40-foot motor fishing vessel *Paragon* set out from Rosslare specially equipped to reap a particular type of seaweed growing off our southeast coast for sale in Norway. The crew was allegedly going to earn a good deal more than from fishing. The venture did not in fact launch a great new industry but it does serve as a reminder that the sea around us is rich in other resources than fish. The exploitation of these resources could be speeded up if we had, as we eventually must have, an overall national maritime policy.

The rest of the decade saw continuous but not rapid progress and the emergence of a growing problem with the obligation lying on all skippers hire-purchasing through BIM (a rapidly rising number) to market most of their catches through that organisation. The system was clumsy and led to friction between wholesalers and BIM (accused of keeping down prices), between fishermen and BIM (accused of preventing fishermen from getting the price they might), and between the industry and the public, convinced that it was paying more for fish than necessary and that the benefit did not go to the primary producer, the fisherman.

The 'tied boat' rule was to be dropped in 1962 but it has to be admitted that a satisfactory solution to the problem of marketing fish at home has not yet been found. Suspicions survive both on the public's part that it has to pay too much and on the fishermen's that he receives too little of what the public pays. How to associate the consumer with the producer for the maximum benefit of both is one of the riddles that the industry has yet to solve. It has always been an irritant — one needs only to read a series of letters addressed to the Dublin papers in the 1950s and 1960s by the Irish Housewives Association. As the demand for fish has grown, the need to achieve a satisfactory answer to the riddle has grown too. Muintir na Mara complained repeatedly in the late 1950s that 'the fishermen have been abandoned by the Board to the ring of fish-buyers' (letter to *The Irish Times* 25 March 1957). This was because, so far as pelagic fish and shellfish were concerned, the obligation to sell through the Board had gone, and Muintir na Mara, worried at the economic power wielded by fish wholesalers, urged the establishment of producer-consumer co-operatives under state patronage.

Quayside fish auction at Castletownbere

In June 1957 Erskine Childers, then Minister for Lands and Fisheries (who had once said to this writer at a Dun Laoghaire Chamber of Commerce dinner that most of the fishing industry's trouble came because 'the fishermen were bloody minded'), made a brave statement when introducing before the Dáil the annual fishery estimates.

My mind is turning towards the belief that a drastic revision of our conceptions in regard to sea fisheries is necessary. . . . We have a good fishing tradition in certain areas but we have no education directed towards fishing as a vocation. I believe we should have that, and that we must have it if we want to produce skippers who can build up our fishing industry. I hope soon to be able to announce that facilities will be provided for acquiring nautical training for fishermen so that none but qualified skippers will be eligible for boats under the h.p. scheme operated by Bord Iascaigh Mhara.

He spoke also of the need for research into fish stocks and fish behaviour, talked of the need for harbour improvement and of our discreditable 'haphazard marketing arrangements', and ended by announcing that fish landings the previous year had for the first time topped £1 million in value, with a sharp increase in values and quantities landed in all categories. Exports of fish exceeded imports by £300,000 — still not sufficient — and the number of full-time fishermen was still falling. This speech at last reflected in high quarters the growing public interest in the industry and growing disquiet about the slowness of its progress.

In the following years there was progress, if still slow, and public opinion was awakening faster. In March 1958 the Maritime Institute held a very successful public meeting which was attended by Erskine Childers, as minister responsible for fisheries, and addressed, among others, by the French Commercial Counsellor, who outlined the successes of the cooperative movement among fishermen in Britanny. The spokesman for the Institute emphasised that while our industry had made a late start in its revival there was no reason why it should miss the tide altogether. The basic aims were a great increase in the amount of fish caught by Irish vessels and greatly developed marketing organisation and technique. The Minister had promised that at last young fishermen would receive training, and a scheme to carry this out at the Haulbowline naval base was soon to be launched. This was a most important step which must be followed up. The Council of the Institute, he said, believed in the principle of group cooperation by fishermen, and evidence was given that cooperative organisations in Britanny, Scotland and Sweden had succeeded in keeping down the price of nets, bait, fuel and other necessities, and in securing longer credit terms. The possibilities of fish canning on a big scale in Ireland, now that we had our own aluminium industry, were discussed. And, as important as training, the need for research, particularly on herring migrations and shoaling patterns round our south and west coasts, was stressed. The Institute at the time was campaigning for the establishment of a national helicopter service, particularly to help the sea rescue service, and it was suggested that helicopters could be used to help fishery research. *Irish Fishing* was putting forward the same proposal. Finally, the need for an Irish aquarium was emphasised by the Institute's speaker. (We still have not got one.) The Institute next ran a series of film shows devoted to sea fishing and inaugurated a 'fish week' to try to get the maximum of publicity for the industry's possibilities.

The total estimates for state expenditure for 1958—9 were £110,002,220, a reduction of more than £2½ million on 1957—8. But significantly the spending programme for fisheries went up from £204,520 to £223,150, still niggardly but, as *Irish Fishing* supposed, no doubt 'wrung drop by drop like blood from the Ministry of Finance' — a tribute to the slowly altering climate of public opinion and its reflection in high places.

In 1958 it was gleefully reported that Cromane mussel fishermen were earning as much as £34 weekly per two-man boat. And more Dunmore herrings were exported through the tra-

ditional outlet of Milford Haven than in any year since the war. In 1959 we still were the only European fishing nation without a fleet of fishing craft of 72 feet and over, but progress continued. The government agreed to spend another £200,000 on improving Killybegs harbour. BIM's quick-freezing plant went into production at Schull, County Cork. Killybegs' fish meal factory, realisation of another of the Maritime Institute's once-scorned dreams, was reported 'working full blast' on pilchards caught by skippers Carr and Duggan off Dunfanaghy. The Arklow trawlers *Glenmalure* and *Glendalough* were catching quantities of whiting outside Dublin bay with a new type of trawl, the vinge. And twenty-two boats lobster fishing

The Glenmalure which used a vinge type trawl

Lobster fishing

off West Cork had a 'bumper season'. The first six months of 1960 saw a rise of 18 per cent in the quantity of demersal fish landed and over 60 per cent for pelagic, nearly 30,000 tons landed in all. Shellfish landed showed a small rise in value and the total value of landings at £700,397 for the six months was up about 20 per cent.

In March 1960 the Maritime Institute closed its most successful winter season of maritime films to date with a presentation of four films lent by BIM from its now growing film library. Its spokesman announced that the Institute would be cooperating in running for the first time a fisheries pavilion at the RDS Spring Show, and that at its premises on St Michael's Wharf, Dun Laoghaire it would stage a fisheries exhibition throughout the summer. Both the pavilion and the exhibition were markedly successful and did much to create a new attitude among younger people towards the industry. The pamphlet *Ireland's Sea Fisheries* which the Institute published in 1960 was quickly sold out. It maintained that we ought to have 10,000 full-time fishermen with 40,000 employed ashore in canning, marinating, boatbuilding, marketing and other ancillary industries; that our home consumption should double again to 25,000 tons and be satisfied by catches by our own fishermen, and that we ought to be able to earn £15 million annually from fish exports, which should rise to 160,000 tons, ten times the current figure. It underlined once again the importance of training and research and called for the injection of more capital into the industry. Demonstrating the value of the expression of public concern in constructive terms through such an organisation as the Institute, the pamphlet recalled that the recent great improvement in the quality of Radio Éireann's broadcast weather forecasts to fishermen and coastal craft was the result of the presentation by the Institute to the government of the findings of prolonged research which it had undertaken into the opinions of trawlermen and coastal skippers.

In 1960 the government publication office issued the detailed proposals of the Swedish harbour consultant, C.G. Bjuke, on the improvement of fishing harbour facilities. This expert, who had been commissioned by the government to examine every Irish fishery port and make proposals, suggested that Howth, Passage East, Kinsale, Castletownbere, Valentia, Galway, Greencastle and above all Killybegs should be developed as rapidly as finances permitted 'to form the nucleus of a developed Irish industry'. The Bjuke report remains well worth studying and its plans and aerial photographs are of very high quality. Bjuke thought the development of the fishing industry a very practical proposition, concluding that it seemed probable 'that the growth of the industry will be such that the eight ports will not satisfy its requirements' and that some of the other ports 'used by inshore fishermen with smaller craft' should not be neglected.

By now Ireland was enforcing a four mile fishing limit drawn from base lines and the need to supplement our inshore fleet with a fleet of middle-water trawlers had become imperative. It was well expressed in an optimistic article by Clayton Love in *Development*, a journal devoted to economic topics which played a part in launching Ireland into the quick-growth era of the 1960s. Clayton Love said that BIM required reconstitution, that fisheries should be removed from the tutelage of the Departments of Lands or Agriculture to that of Industry and Commerce and that a long-term government fisheries policy must be devised. He calculated that the average sea fisherman was earning £220 per annum, and that the average skipper buying a new boat for an average price of between £10,000 and £15,000 was being left, after paying his crew from the £1,800 p.a. which the boat would earn, with only £750 to meet all expenses. He showed that we had, as ever, a hard-working core of good fishermen, but believed they were in danger of being let 'go to seed'. He advocated the creation of 'a producer fleet of wide sea range . . . within strict controls so that its numbers and catching capacity are economically related to our home and export market capacity'. Such expansion, he believed, would be of great benefit rather than a threat to the inshore men, providing him with 'an expanding and more volatile market' while the absence of large trawlers from the four mile area would lead to a build-up of stocks.

The Maritime Institute had held a symposium on the future of the fisheries at the Four Courts Hotel earlier in the year, addressed by Seán de Cleir, Arthur Reynolds, fisheries correspondent of *The Irish Times*, and Nicholas Kervick, a leading figure in the quickly-expanding Dunmore East export trade. Ideas

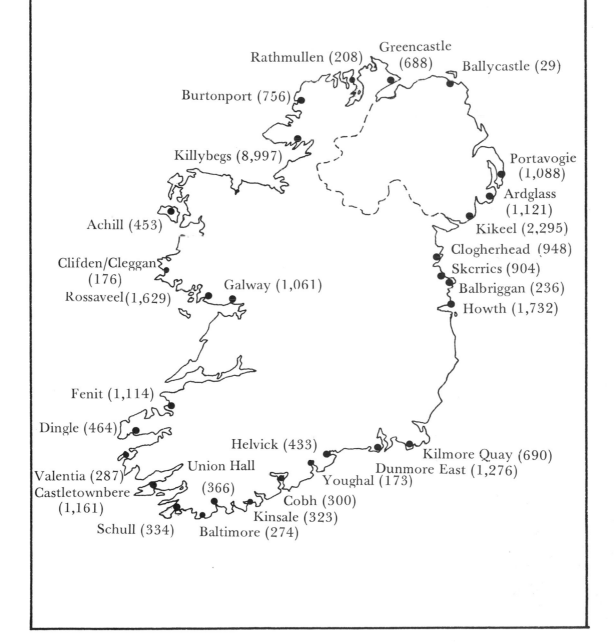

**IRELAND — VALUES OF LANDINGS
AT LEADING PORTS 1980**

*Latest figures available 1980 Republic IR£'000s,
1980 N. Ireland £'000s sterling*

Rathmullen (208)

Greencastle (688)

Ballycastle (29)

Burtonport (756)

Killybegs (8,997)

Portavogie (1,088)

Ardglass (1,121)

Achill (453)

Kikeel (2,295)

Clifden/Cleggan (176)

Clogherhead (948)

Galway (1,061)

Skcrrics (904)

Rossaveel (1,629)

Balbriggan (236)

Howth (1,732)

Fenit (1,114)

Dingle (464)

Helvick (433)

Kilmore Quay (690)

Valentia (287)

Union Hall (366)

Dunmore East (1,276)

Castletownbere (1,161)

Youghal (173)

Cobh (300)

Kinsale (323)

Schull (334)

Baltimore (274)

similar to Clayton Love's had been expressed. It had been noted that of 10,000 tons of whiting caught annually round Ireland, our fishermen took only 3,000 and that mackerel was virtually not being fished at all. Processing plants, it was emphasised, were for long periods insufficiently supplied between gluts. Howth fishermen, it was reported, were now sailing direct into British ports and selling there, a most promising pioneer effort.

The 1960 catch was up 16 per cent in quantity on that of 1959 but not much in value, and the value of shell-fish caught fell. During the year Kinsale-canned herrings became available on the Irish market, and the National Fishermen's Organisation — at the time the most vocal of the many and too ephemeral organisations that have tried, down the years, to act as spokesmen for the fishermen — joined with the Killybegs Fishermen's Association in demanding exemption of fishermen from the newly imposed PAYE tax system. Skerries fishermen formed a cooperative society to market their whiting. During December 1960 five fishermen lost their lives on our coasts. The inadequacy of training in safety techniques and of provision for the dependents of such casualties were widely discussed. One of BIM's three large fishing vessels was still fishing, but the other two were laid up for long stretches for lack of suitable crews. The fishing fleet in 1960 had reached 5,200 tons, mostly vessels between 49 feet and 54 feet, compared with 1,000 tons in 1935 and 2,900 tons when BIM was formed in 1952.

Significant of the growing public interest in the sea fisheries was the debate that took place in 1960 at the annual congress of the Vocational Education Association on a resolution 'that in Vocational Schools in coastal areas steps be taken to interest the students in maritime affairs, e.g. visits to fishing vessels, cargo ships, ports, fish processing plants, etc. and demonstrations to students by experts of maritime and fishing developments, with the object of associating young students with the national drive to develop our merchant and fishing fleets, and that, wherever possible, elementary courses in navigation be instituted'. The resolution came from Dun Laoghaire Vocational Education Committee, which had itself thoroughly debated it and thoroughly briefed its delegation, and this resulted from the activities of the Maritime Institute in that borough. The resolution was carried unanimously and years later Kinsale Technical School pioneered its implementation.

The Standing Council of the Vocation Association met the top officials of the Department of Education early in 1961 and discussed the need to attract 'a better type of boy' into the industry (still so recently considered a dumping ground for undesirables). It was told that 'up to the present the response to the advertisements issued by the Fisheries Branch of the Department of Lands for boys to train as fishermen had been disappointing'. Dun Laoghaire Vocational Committee then submitted a resolution to the 1961 Vocational Education Association's Congress of Kilkee demanding that its previous year's resolution be seriously followed up. Speakers made a detailed and reasoned case for attention by the education authorities and the government as a whole to the fishing industry, and it was unanimously decided to ask Standing Council to take the matter up again and to circularise all vocational education committees about it.

It was time opinion got moving. 1961 was a bad year; the amount and value of the catch fell for the first time for many years. True, the fishing fleet

Cú na Mara — the Department of Agriculture and Fisheries' second research ship following the Cú Feasa. Neither vessel was wholly satisfactory and neither could compare with the former Department of Agriculture and Technical Instruction's Helga I

now topped 5,500 tons and by now the fishery research vessel *Cu Feasa*, discarded in 1978, had begun to operate under BIM's management. But there were too many signs that the industry was marking time after a decade of advance. The value of boats and gear issued by BIM was down, no new boats were taken on by Gaeltacht fishermen on the special terms available to them, production at BIM's fish processing stations at Galway, Killybegs and Schull was reported as 'considerably below capacity' and, though a new ice plant at Castletownbere brought the number run by BIM to nine, 'sales fell far short of potential supply' and there was a heavy loss on the operation of the nine plants. *Irish Fishing* called it 'a disappointing year'; we were 'still far from an important break-through . . . Processing made no major advances'. The same journal wrote:

Allow conservatively £500,000 to run and maintain 194 boats [our fleet at the time] . . . allow £10 per week per man, to include the cost of provisions and loan repayments. This would give the average crewman only £5 or £6 per week. The total cost of the fleet is now:

Running Costs	£500,000
Earnings	£920,920
	£1,420,920

But the boats only earn a total of £1,206,000. So even these very conservative figures would show the fleet failing to pay by about £250,000 a year.

Moreover, Scottish inshore fishermen were earning over £12 a week and 'a good fisherman should not be expected to work for less'.

8

From Stagnation to Achievement: the Irish Fishing Industry from 1962 to 1979

In spite of the critical condition of the industry in 1961, all the public pressure of previous years was having its effect. Early in 1962 Brian Lenihan, then Secretary in charge of Fisheries to the Minister for Lands, issued a white paper announcing a complete reorganisation of the boat loan scheme. The capital grant towards the cost of a new boat was fixed at 25 per cent, more or less on a par at last with the kind of inducements long on offer for new entrants into other spheres of production. The owner who cleared his boat in ten years would get a refund of 10 per cent of the initial cost. Lower interest rates were to be available to all hire-purchasers, covering now for the first time hire-purchase of second-hand vessels. Existing repayment periods were to be extended. It was proposed to quote fish meal prices at the point of landing so as to cut out waste of unmarketable catches and endeavour to prevent price-collapses. A start was to be made on building a new £25,000, 65 foot boat designed by BIM which had already begun building a standard 33 foot boat with 33 hp engine for shell fishermen. BIM was to be reorganised. A special training course was to be opened for boys of sixteen years and over with reasonable educational standards, and men with three years' experience were invited to apply for training as skippers and receipt of certi-

ficates of competency. Trainees in both categories would receive maintenance payments.

The Maritime Institute was particularly pleased with the new training proposals and a deputation from the Institute told Brian Lenihan so, but urged greater provision for research. This was also demanded publicly by the Institute when it published a memorandum on the white paper. Meanwhile it was rumoured that the Taoiseach, Seán Lemass, was taking a personal interest in the industry's future and demanding a radical new approach. James Dillon, speaking for the principal opposition party and formerly the minister responsible for fisheries, was objecting strongly to any project that would expand our fleet into middle waters or further. The government made it clear that it was ready to follow Mr. Bjuke's advice and develop certain major fishing ports. There was a general air of expectation.

In August Brian Lenihan advertised for a new executive to reorganise BIM and propel Irish fishing into the export market on the grand scale. Irishmen took over from foreigners the running of Killybegs fish-meal plant and Dingle fishermen at the end of the year were reporting record catches with the new Larsen mid-water herring trawl. On 30 November, 1962 the Department of Lands announced that Brendan O'Kelly, BComm, already nationally known as originator of the 'Young Farmer of the Year' competition, had been appointed wholetime chairman of BIM. The former, part-time chairman since 1952, Seamus Ó Mealláin, BE, MICEI, was needed to meet expanding work of a technological nature in the Department's Fisheries Division. The new BIM would have novel functions in the advisory and development spheres. This was the inauguration of BIM as we know it. It was quickly to become under an energetic and imaginative chairman capable of attracting colleagues of quality, the principal (though still not the sole) agency for an unprecedentedly rapid growth of the fishing fleet, its catch, fishery exports and consumption, the employment generated in the industry and the public esteem in which it was held.

Coincidentally, the Fishing Industry Development Committee, appointed by the Minister from all areas of the industry, initiated the national fish cookery competition which under BIM's supervision has done so much to increase the quantity and quality of fish consumption at home.

BIM under the new dispensation gave up its participation in the wholesaling of fish. The pros and cons of this decision were fiercely argued at the time, for example by the Howth fishermen's co-operative, and have been since. It is still widely felt that the distribution of fish in the home market is unsatisfactory, the price to the consumer often needlessly high and that received by the fishermen too low. Satisfactory organisation of this side of the industry is achievable but will require much thought and patience and generate a considerable clash of interests.

Meanwhile in 1962 and 1963 distinguished national figures like Peadar O'Donnell (who had been the member of the Population and Emigration

Commission most interested in the evidence submitted by the Maritime Institute) were calling for a more intelligent interest to be taken in our sea fisheries and deploring the unhappy disputes then taking place off the Waterford coast between local and County Down fishermen.

Improvements began to be noted. The government announced its intention to get construction of a new fisheries research ship started before the end of 1964. Dingle fishermen launched a cooperative society. Connemara oyster stocks were reported flourishing, and success was achieved with an experimental oyster bed in Clew bay. *The Irish Times* was sufficiently excited by the prospects to commission in April 1963 four long articles by Arthur Reynolds which gave a masterly summary of the recent history and future possibilities of the industry. BIM began production of the long series of attractive brochures which have done so much to sell both fish and the idea of fish to the Irish public. Irish fishermen began demanding a 12-mile fishery-limit and in the first two months of 1963 landings were up by 130 tons and nearly £33,000 in value on the corresponding period of 1962.

Throughout 1964 there were reports that large deep-sea fleets operated jointly by Irish and foreign interests were going to start fishing from Galway or some other Irish port, but the real growth of the industry occurred with the steady inflow of larger vessels into the existing Irish fleet — the number of boats fishing from Kilmore quay, for instance, rose to twenty-four in January with the arrival of Thomas Power's 72 foot *Alliance*. Early in the year, Wexford fishermen were reporting enhanced herring catches thanks to the research activities of the *Cu Feasa*. But it was evident that one of the industry's

Dunmore East's pier during the herring glut, 1964

chronic weaknesses had not yet been overcome when Dunmore East closed its port owing to the huge herring catch, which could not be disposed of despite a temporary quota restriction of 50 crans a boat. Heavy catches continued to keep prices low — to the fishermen's disadvantage — though not, according to one well-known fish merchant, as low as in Britain. He blamed large imports of foreign canned fish and fish fingers for any problems suffered on the home market. Fishermen's cooperatives throve in 1964, and so did the catching of sand eels off North County Dublin for conversion to fish meal. Fish pro-

cessing began to assume its present sophisticated form at Killybegs.

A noteworthy sign of the approach of the industry towards maturity was the attendance of a party of fishermen from several Irish ports at the World Fishery Exhibition in London in 1963. Another sign in February 1964 was the founding of Ireland's longest-lived maritime journal, *The Irish Skipper*, directed by Arthur Reynolds. The lead story in the first issue declared that Ireland would soon have extended fishing limits; beside it was a photograph of Brian Lenihan and his message of goodwill to the new venture. More important,

Currachs formed an important part of this community's life, on Dingle peninsula

the journal gave prominence to Brendan O'Kelly's statement that 'no major expansion of the fishing industry could take place unless it was based on fuller fishery research'. This statement was made when he gave details of a new joint Irish-US research project. The ninth issue of *The Skipper* reported that Aer Lingus was flying out Irish lobsters to the Continent 'by the ton'. The BIM credit plan giving grants of a quarter of the engine cost to small-boat fishermen wanting to motorise their craft proved most successful. Between 1962 and 1964 108 engines were installed, representing an investment of some £30,000 by fishermen. BIM, surveying its work in this domain, recorded that the currach was fast losing its traditional status as the standard west-coast fishing craft; instead a 26-foot engined lobster boat was preferred, twenty-six of which had recently gone into service between Killala bay and Broadhaven. These, BIM pointed out, had a wider range, were better equipped and safer than the currach, and landed larger catches.

In the first ten months of 1965 catches were up 23 per cent in quantity

Currach building, Maharee Islands, Co. Kerry

and 14 per cent in value on the same period in 1964. Foreign poaching became a serious issue once again and demands were made for replacement of our three obsolete second-world-war corvettes with ships of which our naval service could be proud and which would have the speed to catch modern trawlers poaching. The survey of waters off our coasts by the Polish fishery research ship *Birkut* was a pointer to events soon to come. Ironically, the quite astonishing growth of the fishing industry of Poland — whose modern statehood was more or less contemporary with ours, whose history was similar, but whose coast line was much shorter and further from the main fishing grounds — had frequently been held up as a model for our own fishing industry by the Maritime Institute.

BIM which had sold its three German trawlers was busy congratulat

ing a number of skippers for meeting their hire-purchase commitments before time; it was also expanding the fish processing industry. When the US research team issued its report the Maritime Institute again set up a subcommittee to consider it and prepare a memorandum. This (issued in November 1964 and much publicised in 1965) welcomed the team's plea (following Bjuke) for the small fishing port dependent on small boat, inshore fishermen, both on sociological grounds and because their product was usually of the best quality. It also repeated its demand for ever more basic research and endorsed the policy of penetrating in a big way into the middle-waters area.

In 1965 a new government (but of the same political complexion) transferred fisheries from Lands back to Agriculture. The Maritime Institute was demanding a Department of Marine

Part of the fleet of lobster boats for the North Mayo coast undergoing sea trials in Dingle, Co. Kerry. The fleet of 21 vessels was built at BIM boatyards in Dingle, Baltimore and Killybegs in the 1960s

to supervise all maritime development, mercantile, fishing and military, with facilities for initiating the long-awaited Irish hydrographic survey, first strongly urged by the 1930 Ports and Harbours Tribunal. (At the time of writing there has still been no move to institute a national hydrographic service). 1965 was also the year when, after years of decline, fishing began to revive at Bantry, and Greencastle received five 50-foot vessels. In autumn 1965 the government introduced, 'temporarily', a 12-mile limit with special concessionary zones for trawlers of nations that 'traditionally' had fished those areas. Fishermen's co-operatives ran a much praised display stand at the Associated Countrywomen of the World conference in Dublin. The Maritime Institute continued to show fishery films to the public, and one on the latest Japanese fishing techniques aroused wide comment. The Kilkeel fishing fleet had the best year in its history, and no fewer than eight young Ballyhack, County Wexford, fishermen received their skipper's certificates. The Food and Agricultural Organisation reported in 1965 that the 1963 world catch had risen to a record 51.6 million tons.

Early in 1966 the Dublin papers were enlivened by a long controversy about the state of the fishing industry. It was evident that catching power had greatly increased but the increase in demersal fish landings by 1,750 tons between 1964 and 1965 and by a further 750 tons in 1965 was considered insufficient, especially when set beside a sharp decline in the catch of pelagic fish. What the critics of BIM failed to see was that the fall off in landings of pelagic fish were, at that stage, attributable mainly to inadequate research — insufficient knowledge of the habits of the erratic herring — insufficient training, and neglect of the once much sought

mackerel. BIM may have failed to make a case sufficiently vigorously on these three points, but they were all matters on which it was showing growing concern, and what it had done since its reconstitution was to ensure the existence in future of an Irish middle-waters fishing fleet whose landings would be able to guarantee an end to perennial vast fluctuations in supply, especially in bad weather. BIM in its new form also had its eyes firmly fixed on the necessity to drive up exports; this it was soon to accomplish. Indeed, in June 1966 Brendan O'Kelly was telling the conference of the Institute of Journalists that overseas orders had out-stripped the capacity of the Irish fleet while the home market was steadily growing. What a change from the days of the Sea Fisheries Association, and still more from the disastrous first decade of the industry after the break from Britain.

In May 1966 Ireland's first stern-trawler *Miss Trudel* was launched at St Malo in France for a Cork company. With a length of 110 feet and an 800 hp engine driving her at 12 knots, she was a revolutionary entrant into our fleet. (Trawling directly over the ship's stern instead of over the quarter was a post-second-world-war technique — easier and more efficient.) The idea of companies, or the state, operating trawlers along with — or, as it was asserted, in competition with — the skipper-owner was still anathema to some observers of the scene and to some involved in it. The new £40,000, 65-foot fishery research vessel *Cu na Mara*, built at BIM's Killybegs yard, came into service in the summer of 1966. Half a million pounds worth of fishing craft had been constructed at this yard since 1952, and Killybegs with a fleet of thirty fishing craft manned by 150 fishermen was making an annual catch worth £300,000. In 1966 one of the industry's

Miss Trudel, Ireland's first stern trawler

best known skippers of recent years, Brian Crummey of Dun Laoghaire, skipper since 1959 of the 56-foot *Ard Ailbhe*, discarded her for the 66-foot Swedish *Nordkap* with her 205 hp, supercharged engine — another pointer to the growth in size of the average vessel fishing from Irish ports. The new Killybegs-built 56-foot *Ard Scia* was handed over to an Aran fisherman, Ciaran Gill of Killeany, in September 1966 — Aran was becoming very different from what it had been till even decades after Synge. Coincidentally, it was in 1966 that Dr. A.E.J. Went, scientific adviser to the Department of Fisheries, told a meeting of the Royal Irish Academy the story of the rise, progress and recent demise of the

Aran basking shark fishery, chronicled in the 1930s by Robert Flaherty in *Man of Aran*, a classic among fishing films.

Criticism early in 1967 in *The Irish Times* of 'the high cost of growth in our fishing industry' was convincingly answered in a letter from Arthur Reynolds, and more convincingly still by the publication on 11 January of the Department of Agriculture's statistics for fish landings in 1965 — £200,000 more valuable than in 1964 at just over £1.7 million and nearly 11,000 tons more in quantity. Twelve Greencastle fishermen received the skipper's certificate in February 1967, and in April Brendan O'Kelly was able to announce, at the presentation of prizes for the annual fish cookery competition, that consumption at 10 lbs per head of the population had shot up 33 per cent in four years. In May, Albert Swan of Killybegs acquired the £40,000, 75-foot *Mallrin,* equipped with the new sonar for fish detection and with radar and automatic pilot. His sonar could detect fish at a distance of up to 1,250 yards, a prodigious innovation. He was reputed to have been, in his previous ship *Christine*, (paired with *Radiance,* also of Killybegs) Ireland's most successful herring catcher. The pair several times caught 100 tons in a day. The growing popular interest in fish was manifested in May 1967 by the success of a four-day sea food festival in Howth.

National consumption of fish rose again this year to an average of 11.2 lbs per head.

In the autumn came a long awaited announcement, that a fishmeal plant would be built at Mornington on the Boyne estuary capable of coping with 35,000 tons of fish in a year. Meanwhile *The Skipper* had been campaigning against the regulation which banned Irish trawlers of over 100 tons gross or 400 hp engine from fishing within the 12-mile limit. Growth seemed more important than conservation those twelve short years ago. Today *The Skipper*, like BIM and the Maritime Institute, is optimistic enough to believe both are possible. In August 1967 Seaborn Ltd

The bridge of a modern trawler. The complexity of the equipment now carried (radar, sonar, decca navigator, radio telephony etc.) explains the need for the best possible training for those taking charge of our most modern fishing vessels

The mussel purification plant at Cromane, Co. Kerry

became the first company in the food-processing field in Ireland to be licensed to use the standard mark of the Institute for Industrial Research and Standards. This was hailed as 'a real breakthrough for Irish fish processing' in *The Irish Times*.

Fish landings in the first half of 1967 were up 10 per cent in value and demersal landings some 25 per cent in quantity compared with January to June 1966. The long-successful BIM mussel purification centre at Cromane (opened first in 1940) was handed over by BIM to the Castlemaine Harbour Fishermen's Co-operative, and a serious campaign was started to restore the Irish oyster industry to its past importance. Also, a bill was introduced before the Dáil for the establishment, development, operation and management of five major fishing harbours — Castletownbere, Howth, Killybegs, Galway and Dunmore East (instead of Passage East as Proposed by Bjuke). In February 1968 Neil Blaney, Minister for Agriculture and Fisheries, reported that the 1966 catch had for the first time exceeded £2 million and fish exports nearly £2½ million. The catch for the first eleven months of 1967 had been up on that for the corresponding months of 1966, and harmonious relations had been restored with the County Down fishermen. The training course for skippers, held at Galway Vocational School in those years, was more and more popular.

In March 1968 Brendan O'Kelly launched what may in the end prove to be the most constructive idea of all on building the industry (tentatively put up in 1949 by the Maritime Institute, as already recorded): that the future might well lie primarily with the development of fish farming. He was speaking at the Irish Universities Biological Congress. The Lett-Doran Company of Wexford took delivery of a £60,000, 80 foot, elaborately equipped, steel trawler built in Poland. BIM had now agreed with Norway, France and Poland favourable credit terms for Irish fishermen buying vessels in those countries and fore-shadowed increased purchases by those countries of Irish fish products. In June it was reported that the £2 million invested in fishing since 1964 was now assuring a much more steady supply, and so encouraging investment in ancillary industries ashore likely to provide employment.

There were, however, problems. A number of large foreign trawlers, chiefly German, had been arrested by the ancient corvettes for poaching inside our limits, and many more were known to have got away. Skin-diving was reported to be interfering in several areas with shell-fishing and some unpleasant incidents had occurred. The Galway fish plant had to close in controversial circumstances. Above all, there was still need for more extensive research.

The research question was sharply raised at an impressive symposium on fisheries organised by the Cork Scientific Council in October 1968. Along with John Courlander, now the Institute's honorary curator, the present writer represented the Maritime Institute. On behalf of the Institute he warned that Ireland was falling behind its competitors in fishery research. He told the symposium that in France, for instance, a purchase tax of 2 per cent was now levied on all fish used in canning, the proceeds going exclusively to sea fisheries research; the French industry, moreover, already had an astonishingly detailed knowledge of Irish waters. In Britain more emphasis was also being placed on fisheries research, and the White Fish Authority there had recently set up a fully equipped industrial development unit to measure performance at sea with a view to better exploitation of the industry's resources.

He said that in Ireland some useful research was already being undertaken but much more needed to be done. The current investigation into the habits of the Dunmore East herring would be of great long-term value but there was also a pressing need for short-term projects. The Institute thought it would be worthwhile to equip a ship to search for herring outside the normal season, say in April, and at a location not before fished for herring. Another area where research was needed was in the training and use of manpower. There was also scope for greatly increased market research. Ireland did not appreciate the vast size of the international market for fish and how fast it was growing. The Maritime Institute now considered that there should be an annual target of £10 million of fish exports. Output on this level would eventually support an industry employing 10,000 full-time fishermen, backed by another 40,000 employees in ancillary industries

Construction work at Dunmore East port, about 1968

ashore. The key to all future development lay in spending more money now on research, the Institute was convinced. Following extensive research into shell-fish farming in France, that part of the French industry was now worth more than £30 million annually. Full development of Ireland's own shell-fish resources could transform the coastal economies of Cork and Kerry.

Among many speakers, Professor Keady of the Marine Biology Department at University College, Galway, spoke of the threat of pollution to fish stocks; criticised the fact that BIM had been able to appoint only two biologists, and that recently; maintained that the *Cu Feasa* had turned out to be a poor research ship while the *Cu na Mara* was too small; pointed out that a National Marine Research Centre had been promised for Galway but the promise had not been fulfilled; and accused the Fisheries Branch of the Department not only of lacking basic equipment but of opposing UCG's proposal that a shellfish laboratory be set up at Carna with a small research vessel attached. Tom Geoghegan of BIM explained how shellfish exports had gone up from £825,000 in value in 1963 to £1.5 million in 1967, 45 per cent going to Britain, 25 per cent to France and 9 per cent to the Netherlands. He also observed that while salted herring exports were being developed again, more fish was being handled locally instead of having to go through the Dublin market, and crab meat was now being produced at Schull.

What was still evident at this stage in the development of the industry was the absence of close co-operation and consultation between those directing it, nominally the Department of Agriculture, those doing research for it and the fishermen themselves. In time the officers of BIM came to see the essential importance of such co-operation and consultation, and it is largely to their credit, though also to that of the fishermen who were growing more confident and more soundly organised, that co-operation and consultation are, at the time of writing, much more satisfactory.

It was in 1968 that the leading British fishery journal, *Fishing News,* wrote of our industry being 'gripped firmly in a development programme', and of Ireland 'turning to fisheries development with the zest that she once poured into politics. She is rediscovering her natural wealth . . . and has just begun to understand how valuable her rich fishing waters could be'. The British journal praised BIM for its recent policy of toughness over hire-purchase repayments, leading sometimes to repossession of boats and their reissue to keener, young skippers.

In the first two months of 1969 wet fish landings were one-third higher than in the first two months of 1968, and growth was really seen to be occurring. The political parties begun to realise that they would now have to show an interest in the industry, and the Labour Party incorporated a special fishery section into the maritime policy which it issued as part of its over-optimistic programme for 'the Socialist Seventies'. Its proposals, as the *Irish Press* was quick to point out, closely resembled those of the National Federation of Fishermen's

Co-operatives, including improved training facilities, more long- and short-term research, greater powers for BIM and stimulation of the formation of producing and marketing co-operatives. At the same time the *Irish Independent* pointed out that, after an encouraging start, lack of proper planning was seriously delaying the plan for establishing five major fishing ports.

By the end of 1969, in which year fish-product exports reached a record £3 million, there were seventeen registered fishery co-operatives round the coast. Their turnover was estimated at at least £750,000, and the number of shareholders at over 700. There were record herring landings at Galway and Dunmore East. In December a Danish coaster left Sligo for Boulogne in France with 3,000 barrels of salted herrings, the first such shipment from Sligo for perhaps centuries. At the same time Brendan O'Kelly, at a two-day conference to brief marine-engine makers on the needs of the Irish fishing industry, foretold a fleet of 1,000 Irish powered fishing craft over 30 feet long by the end of 1972.

Another change in the whole atmosphere of the industry was signalled when BIM put forward proposals for a pension scheme for fishermen. But the Dáil debate in May 1970 on the Sea Fisheries (Amendment) Bill, 1970, designed to increase BIM's borrowing powers (though over £1¼ million had been repaid or written off), showed that politicians who for decades had had very little to say about the industry, were now acutely conscious of its new public image. A Labour deputy pressed for better training facilities for fishermen and declared that the chief advantages gained from the industry's expansion went to 'rings' who kept prices artificially high. A Fine Gael deputy said they were being asked to give £2 million to BIM but they should be giving £10 million. A Fianna Fáil

Fish for export travelling by container

deputy complained that it was still true that in time of plenty the fish caught by our fishermen 'had to be sold at give-away prices'.

Poaching by foreign trawlers continued and fines imposed when they were caught were derisory — less than £100. The press enjoyed itself at the expense of the unfortunate corvettes, all of which were at one time out of action, so that the diminutive *Cu Feasa* had to be impressed to act as fishery protector. At last in June 1970 the government announced that it proposed to acquire three new 'all-weather protection vessels'. During the same month the Naval Association, veterans of the 'emergency' years at sea, held a

wine and sea-food party at Dun Laoghaire at which Brendan O'Kelly declared bluntly that to achieve its full potential the industry would need more capital investment and more skilled manpower.

Later in 1970 BIM gave notice that grants would henceforth be available for pilot projects in fish-farming. This was one of the most important steps BIM had ever taken, the true value of which will only be apparent many years hence. The announcement won immediate public approbation from one of the most persistent and practical critics of government maritime policy, former seamen's union leader Desmond Branigan, who undertook a prolonged investigation of the Clarinbridge oyster industry with his organisation, Marine Research. In November 1970 Brendan O'Kelly followed this up, at a meeting of the Federation of Marine Industries, with a pungent call for more research into the possibilities of fish-farming. Jack Tyrrell, the Arklow boat-builder and president of the Federation, praised BIM for 'producing a prospering fishing industry with a consequent demand for boats'.

The value of landings in 1970, including shellfish, was £3.8 million, £0.8 million up on 1969. Dunmore East had become one of Europe's leading herring ports.

It was about this time that concern began to be expressed in many quarters about the effect on the industry of our entry into the EEC, then being canvassed. Many who might otherwise have favoured it supported the opposition movement out of fear that the clause in the Treaty of Rome permitting fishing craft from EEC member state to fish up the very estuarial waters of each other would lead to flotillas of German, Dutch and French vessels flocking into our coastal waters.

The international importance of the fishing industry was brought home to the Irish people in 1971 by the staging of the biennial World Fisheries Exhibition for the first time in Ireland. This was a great achievement on the part of BIM. Many sophisticated vessels visited Dun Laoghaire — most memorable, perhaps, a superbly equipped German research ship, *Frithjof* — and thousands of fishermen and business people interested in fish products. A sea food festival was held in the Borough to coincide with the exhibition, and Great Southern Hotels as a result now run there one of the most appreciated sea food restaurants in Europe, but by no means the only one in Ireland. Yet in the late 1960s the Maritime Institute had still been deploring the absence of seafood restaurants in the country.

Ironically, the *Irish Press* reported that during the exhibition 'flat fish were particularly scarce, and salmon also' in the Dublin market. Perhaps enterprising entrepreneurs in Dun Laoghaire had diverted them all there. A critical Cork fish merchant took the opportunity to compare in the papers Denmark's fishery preformance and ours — our annual catch 54,000 tons, theirs over a million; our catch value under £4 million; theirs £30 million; our fish product exports £4½ million, theirs £50 million; price of plaice per stone in Ireland 40s., in Denmark 20s. He had to ask who was codding whom.

During the exhibition fishermen from Ireland, England, Wales and the Isle of Man met to coordinate opposition to the fishery policy of the EEC, a subject arousing more and more controversy, then and in the coming months, in the press and on radio and television. In the end even the strictly non-political and very cautious Maritime Institute adopted a resolution condemning the effect on the fishing industry of the terms of entry which we ultimately accepted, despite continuous lobbying by fishermen's organisations and warnings of possible problems to come from the leadership of BIM. Both the Maritime Institute and *The Skipper* asserted that if only we already had a mature fishing industry we would have little to fear from the fleets of future EEC partners, while the foreign poachers that were more and more in the news in the early 1970s would have had much less temptation to infiltrate into grounds already adequately fished. An article in the *Evening Press* on 2 June, 1971 posed the EEC problem starkly. It was about Kilmore Quay where the modern fishermen's co-operative movement had started back in 1955. In 1969 the co-operative's

The opening of Kilmore Quay cooperative, 1955

turnover had been £90,000 in 1970 it was up to £155,000. This village of 225 people was reckoned to earn £240,000 annually from the industry; where would it be if Ireland joined the EEC without having negotiated adequate protection beforehand for our inshore fishermen? Just such protection, according to the article, the Minister for Foreign Affairs, Dr Patrick Hillery, had in fact promised to secure during the entry negotiations.

Throughout 1971 a clamour was kept up to try to force our negotiators to stick out for retention by Ireland on entry to the EEC of its recently acquired 12-mile limit. In the meantime, however, fishing went on. Three Wexford trawlers in a fortnight during the summer netted sea-mines, relics of the anti-submarine barrages laid by the British Navy in two world wars, and reminders of the ever-present perils besetting the sea-fisherman.

The National Science Council held an impressive symposium in the summer of 1971 in Dublin on the potential of the country's maritime economy. Brendan O'Kelly gave a masterly exposition of the growth and prospects of the fishing industry. The symposium led to an invitation to a number of foreign experts to travel round Ireland and assess our maritime potential. After they had done so the delegates to the 1971 symposium were summoned to hear them answer a number of questions put to them by civil servants attached to the various departments concerned with maritime affairs. This meeting disappointed many of those present because the scope for discussion was severely restricted. Far-ranging discussion would seem to be a pre-requisite for harmonious progress in a democratic society.

In August 1971 the Marine Biology Department at UCG was asked by the Galway-Mayo Regional Development Group to carry out a survey to determine

c'est bon...
c'est du poisson
c'est frais...
c'est Irlandais

Bord Iascaigh Mhara/Irish Sea Fisheries Board, Dublin, Ireland

Advertising Irish fish abroad

the richest fishing grounds off the west coast — proof that the persistent stress on the importance of research by BIM, *The Skipper* and the Maritime Institute had begun to affect thinking people not closely associated with fishing.

BIM staged a comprehensive exhibit of Irish fish at the Cologne Food Fair in September 1971, which would have been inconceivable, and impossible, only ten years before.

In November 1971 Dr R.I. Currie,

director of the Scottish Marine Biological Association, told a meeting in the RDS that present fishing methods were really obsolete. The solution would be to apply the methods of modern agriculture to fishing. Intensive fish-farming would enormously increase the world supply of fish. This was what the amateurs of the Maritime Institute had been saying since 1949, and Brendan O'Kelly, the industry's professional leader, for almost ten years.

A typical new addition to the fishing fleet in 1971 was the 70-foot trawler *Anna Maria II*, bought under BIM's agreement with Norway from that country by Frank Scallon of Kilmore Quay on hire purchase at £60,000. This brought the Kilmore fleet up now to twenty-eight, and was to help the local co-operative supply the customers it had acquired as far away as Italy and Czechoslovakia. Another co-operative, in Dun Laoghaire, opened its own fish shop at this time. Unfortunately, after an encouraging start, it failed. It is as well to recall that the industry's undeniable progress in the past seventeen years has been chequered with drownings of fishermen, bankruptcies of boat-owners, disputes between skippers and hands, as between producers and sellers, and business failures like that in Dun Laoghaire. Some of these unhappy events were avoidable, some the consequence of the way the industry had grown in Ireland, some due to decline in stocks, a few perhaps even to 'bloody-mindedness'. But can progress ever be secured without victims along the way?

The early months of 1972 were noteworthy for the growing acrimony over the terms eventually accepted by the Irish negotiators for entry to the EEC. The chairman of the Killala Bay Fishermen's Co-Operative said on 16 January that 'the EEC talks concluded by Dr Hillery were not worth twopence'. A

letter in the *Sunday Independent* of 12 March called the terms 'intolerable'. This feeling was widespread but in its nineteenth annual report issued in March, BIM recorded 'satisfaction' with the terms of the agreement. It has, of course, been in force now for six years, with modifications achieved by arduous negotiation in 1978 by Brian Lenihan, then Minister for Fisheries. Today the problems of the industry are not so much overwhelming penetration of EEC trawlers into our coastal waters, which has been largely avoided, but problems of diminution of certain species, lack of a coherent EEC fishery policy aimed at genuinely helping the weaker members, and the perennial absence of sufficient research to guide the next stop forward.

In April 1972 the Department of Agriculture released its fishery report for 1971. The catch was up 7 per cent on 1970. Exports of fish and fish products had risen 22 per cent to £5.6 million, thus topping the original targets set, admittedly when inflation was far less acute, by the Maritime Institute. By now there were 1,964 full-time fishermen, a very slow but steady growth over recent years, with 3,897 fishing part-time and at least 2,000 people were employed ashore in ancillary industries. The number of boats fishing was around 2,000, but by no means all were over 30 feet. We still had, and have, far to travel to attain the goals set by the Maritime Institute, Seán de Cleir and others in 1959 and 1960, particularly regarding the development of employment in ancillary industries ashore.

The Northern Ireland fisheries had been growing steadily more productive in the 1960s — the value of the catch rose from £197,461 in 1961 to £477,267 in 1967. A 173 page book on the fisheries of Northern Ireland by A.I. Hughes, issued in 1970 by the Minister for

Agriculture in Northern Ireland (their fishermen likewise subject to a farming ministry), was able to show with justifiable pride that landings per hour worked were higher from Northern Irish than from English fishing craft, with the greater effectiveness of the County Down and County Antrim men the more clearly emphasised when the disparity in size between their craft and the average English fishing vessel was taken into account. During these years Kilkeel had overtaken Portavogie as the port with the highest value of landings, and by 1967 forty-one boats were operating from there, four of them over 70 feet long. An operational subsidy had been provided for the Northern fishing fleet since 1960, in the hope that by 1970 it would be wholly viable without state support.

By the 1970s the subsidy was no longer paid to the Northern Ireland fleet, though certain grants and loans were available. In 1974 there were over 600 full-time and some 200 part-time fishermen using 290 boats in Northern Ireland, 119 of them of between 40 feet and 80 feet in length and one over 80 feet. The 1973 catch had been valued at £2,792,848, six times what it had been in 1967. About a third, sometimes rather more, of the Northern Ireland catch is landed directly in the Isle of Man or mainland Britain. The value of the famous Northern Ireland eels caught rose to £804,000 in 1973; the quantity rose from 1,418,000 lb in 1969 to 1,755,000 lb in 1973. Thus, it can be seen that the fishing industry of our kinsmen across the border was also making strides and its fishermen were keeping alive the age-old tradition of Irish fishing expertise. The North runs a Fisheries Research Laboratory at Coleraine and has been operating a regular fishery research programme since 1962 (oddly, the year of BIM's reorganisation), strengthened by a Fisheries Act of 1966 permitting the acquisition and restocking of large stretches of inland waters. There were twelve full-time workers at Coleraine in 1972 and the activities of scientists like Dr Jasper Pearson and Dr Cragg-Hine have won attention from many quarters.

The Fisheries' Research Laboratory at Coleraine, Co. Derry, whose extensive sound research has been carried on in support of Northern Ireland's highly productive fishing fleet

In 1972 in the west of Ireland a 75 per cent government grant was obtained for a £¼ million fishery development scheme in the Broadhaven region, where there has always been a fishing tradition. It was calculated at the time that there were 300 whole-time and 1,000 part-time fishermen in Counties Mayo and Galway. A fish-processing plant for Ballyglass was part of this deal. During the year fish and fish product exports reached a new record value of £7.7 million and the Department declared that landings had risen 276 per cent, home consumption 40 per cent and exports 351 per cent in ten years.

The 1973 national seafood cookery competition received unprecedented publicity. The *Sunday Press* of 13 May devoted a whole page to the presentation ceremony, with photographs of all the finalists and of the parliamentary secretary to the Minister for Finance presenting the trophy to the winner, Anne O'Donnell of Galway. Fish was certainly no longer a dreaded penitential dish in Ireland.

Among the problems looming in 1973 was a growing awareness that herring stocks were sharply diminishing in the Celtic Sea south of Ireland, almost but not quite certainly from over-fishing, particularly by Dutch and French vessels. We were still catching only some 11 per cent of all fish caught in the waters round Ireland and, with the herring moving into the category of luxury fish, the need became apparent for a return to serious fishing of the neglected mackerel, and also for serious consideration of the possibilities of exploiting hitherto unconsidered fish species. If we could get in on this before other nations' fishing fleets, or at least contemporaneously with them, the decline of traditional species might not be a catastrophe. With agreed conservation measures the traditional species would eventually reappear in any case, and more research might find them in hitherto untested areas. This was the period when we began to hear about the blue whiting.

This and other problems of 1973 and succeeding years have clearly shown the need for an ever greater flexibility in the industry. Fishermen must be prepared to experiment with new techniques and to set about chasing new species. The marketing side of the industry has to undertake to persuade the public to eat types of fish to which it is not used, possibly more palatable but likely to be rejected out of perfectly natural conservatism by the potential buyer. All the time education and training in all branches of the industry must improve, new markets must be sought and more research must be carried out. The fishing industry, static and conservative for centuries, has to be dynamic and revolutionary or else it will die. The Japanese, Poles, Russians and others had learned this already; by 1973 it had become the obligatory lesson in Ireland as well.

It was in 1973 that BIM predicted a coming boom in mackerel catches, which it would help bring about; landings in West Cork topped £250,000 worth in the last few months of the year. Processed at Castletownbere, Kenmare and Cork the mackerel were exported to the West Indies, Holland, Belgium, France and Germany. The importers in the latter country declared that Ireland was delivering mackerel 'of outstanding quality'.

BIM's Killybegs yard launched in November for an Aran skipper a 78-foot trawler, the largest wooden trawler ever built in Ireland. A few years before the latest in trawlers was costing £40,000 to £50,000; this 128-ton, 11-knot *Azure Sea* cost £116,000.

At the end of October a disaster occurred when four fishermen were drowned six miles out from Skerries in the Trawler *St Ibar*. Not long after-

The Emer Marie, 86.5 feet, one of the largest wooden hulled trawlers ever built in Ireland

wards the Maritime Institute issued a statement urging all fishermen to make sure their vessels were fully equipped with all regulation safety gear in first class condition. The distress caused by this disaster was one of the reasons prompting BIM to ask Commodore McKenna, till recently head of the Naval Service, to draw up a pamhlet on safety at sea. This, issued the following year under that very title, remains essential reading for every sea fisherman and anyone going to sea in a small boat. Meanwhile the Naval Service, which was kept busy throughout 1973 arresting poaching trawlers of several nationalities, had at last discarded the old corvettes and acquired three small minesweepers and the custom-built fishery protection cruiser *Deirdre*. To these would shortly be added a former Irish Lights tender

renamed *Setanta* and, temporarily while new and improved *Deirdres* were building, a hired foreign vessel.

Another encouraging development in 1973 was the construction of a new fishery training college at Greencastle, County Donegal. Not perhaps the ideal location, this college, which has gradually acquired much sophisticated equipment, was to supersede Galway Vocational School for training trawler skippers and to undertake the training of most of the new recruits. The Nautical College at Dun Laoghaire, which had trained some skippers, was shortly to be moved, despite protests from the Maritime Institute and its own staff, to Cork where it at first experienced difficulties which prevented a steady inflow of would-be trawler skippers. Illustrative of the administrative frustrations which have

LE Deirdre, the first custom built vessel of the Irish Naval Service used in fishery protection

Rossaveal, Co. Galway, a fishing port of growing importance

been a permanent irritant in all branches of our maritime economy, the ultimate authority over the fishery college was (till 1979) to be the Department of Agriculture, but that for the Nautical College was the Department of Education. (With the inauguration of the Greencastle college, training at Haulbowline, which had never been satisfactory but had been a lot better than nothing, came to an end.)

It was in 1973 that a £360,000 pier at Rossaveal, first promised thirty years before and promised again during election campaigns, was at last begun. Rossaveal soon became the chief fishing port on Galway Bay. Among innumerable projects concerned with fishing that hit the headlines for a while and then sank without trace was the project expensively prepared in 1973 for setting up a vertically-integrated (catching, processing and selling) 'Irish International Trawling Company' in Cork. This published a formidable list of 'consultants and sources of information' and a very practical programme of proposed operations.

In 1974 Irish fishermen landed fish to a value of £8.7 million, 17 per cent more than in 1973. Exports were up to £12.3 million, well above the target suggested by the Maritime Institute in 1968. But the volume caught fell slightly from 1973's record 85,700 tons — a figure quite unthinkable only thirty or even twenty years before — to 84,600 tons. However, the industry's contribution to the state's gross national product went up by £3.8 million, or 19.7 per cent, to £23 million. Ireland's fisheries were now contributing more to the gross domestic product than those of any other EEC country save Denmark. This was a proud boast to be able to make.

BIM ran local training courses throughout 1974 to supplement what was on offer at the colleges. Fourteen fishermen won Skipper (Limited) certificates and forty-one won various grades of Second Hand certificates. In the first nine months of 1974 eleven new vessels were brought into the fleet under arrangements with BIM, nine built in Ireland and two in Holland, representing a capital value of about £1.7 million. The Killybegs yard, for a long time exceptionally busy, was turning out high class wooden trawlers. Unhappily, however, the day of the large, middle-waters wooden trawler was dying and no provision was being made, through no discernible fault of BIM's, for BIM's yards to be converted to building with steel. Seven steel trawlers of from 86 feet to 128 feet were on order at the end of 1974 from Swedish, French, British and Dutch yards, and seventeen wooden craft of from 56 feet to 80 feet at home.

The *Irish Independent* stated in a feature article on 20 February that our fishing fleet was 'the most vital in Europe'. Again, what a difference from the press treatment accorded the industry twenty years earlier. The fleet was said now to consist of 400 trawlers and 1,800 inshore craft, employing 6,000, of whom half full-time (these were approximations) and giving employment to 3,000 ashore.

People were beginning to realise, on newspapers at home and in the head offices of foreign fishing fleets, that the waters around Ireland held the only fishing grounds left in Europe which were not seriously overexploited. Thoughtful people at home who saw this point began the long and still continuing battle to ensure that we would take advantage of the situation that had arisen to guarantee for ourselves a far higher proportion of the catch in our region and the position of main fish processor for the EEC.

Fishery executives in Eastern Europe,

The National Fishery Training Centre, Greencastle, Co. Donegal. The Bord Iascaigh Mhara mobile training unit is parked in front

already no doubt well informed through the findings of the Polish research ship *Birkut* in 1965 (page 129), decided to send huge fleets to fish off Ireland while the long heralded Law of the Sea Conference was wrangling about the right of states or groups of states to declare a 200-mile exclusive limit. (The EEC declared a 200-mile limit a few months later.) In consequence, 1974 was a year when Soviet, Romanian, Bulgarian and Polish trawlers, with the most advanced equipment and accompanied by large factory ships, descended upon this region. Several vessels from these fleets ran foul of our diminutive fishery patrol ships. Some, not without drama, were arrested and brought into Irish ports. One, arrested by L.E. *Grainne* under Lieutenant-Commander J. Jordan, had to pay the customary derisory fine of £75, and had catch and gear, worth nearly £100,000, confiscated. She was

eventually let go on payment of £60,000. (Such monies ought by law to be made over for fishery research.)

The Clarinbridge oyster beds had been handed over by BIM to a co-operative. It was doing well, and enabled Galway to run a record oyster festival in September to mark its twinning contract with the French fishing port of L'Orient.

It became necessary to impose temporary bans on herring fishing in the Mourne Fishery, off Counties Down, Louth and North Dublin, to combat stock depletion. This together with uncertainty about EEC fishery policy — most of those concerned with the industry were demanding for Ireland an exclusive 50-mile limit within the EEC 200-mile limit — led a substantial number of fishermen to open the campaign, victoriously concluded three years later, for a separate Minister and Department of Fisheries. It was from this time on that the public, and others, began to understand the vigour and sense of purpose pervading the recently formed Irish Fishermen's Organisation, now the recognised champion of the skipper-owners of our middle-waters fleet.

In 1975 Irish fishermen landed sea and shellfish to the value of £10.5 million. As much as £1.4 million worth was landed fresh by Irish fishermen in ports in other countries — a healthy recent development. Exports increased by 12 per cent to £13.77 million, excluding the fish landed directly overseas. Once more the industry's contribution to the gross national product was

up 16 per cent to £26.7 million. £4.5 million was invested in the fleet, more than twice as much as in 1974. The fleet now numbered 2,006 craft under 50 feet, 280 more than ten years before; 175 between 51 feet and 65 feet, 25 more; 106 between 66 feet and 72 feet, 73 more; 57 between 73 feet and 90 feet, 54 more; and two over 90 feet, unknown in 1965.

BIM's report for 1975 included a useful table showing that in 1973 some 782,000 tons of fish had been caught in sea areas contiguous to Ireland, excluding salmon. We caught about 11 per cent of this and the Scots and French were the chief catchers in the

Hauling in a catch

area; so for all our progress, and the 82,00 tons or so we were catching, we had much to do, as we still have, to be able confidently to claim a decisive role in planning the future fishing policy governing such coveted and prolific fishing grounds. This was the muscle we lacked when punching at Brussels that year for the right to an exclusive 50-mile limit.

In April 1975 Irish fishermen staged a temporary blockade of six major ports to try to force our government to put up a stronger fight on the question of fishing limits, and also to try to induce the government to institute a fuel subsidy and work out a coherent plan for development of our fishery resources. None of these aims was attained but the very widespread public sympathy for the protesters showed that the industry had at last won back the kind of place in the hearts of Irish people that it evidently held in our fishing ports in the Middle Ages, and never since.

Belfast and Warrenpoint were blocked by Northern Ireland fishermen at the same time, as part of a protest by fishermen from all sections of the industry in Britain against what were looked on as threats by the EEC to give continental fishing fleets a free hand to fish in British waters. The continentals were considered to have over-exploited their own seas and now to be wanting to do the same in the seas off these islands. Irish fishermen started emphasising that if this country did not make claims on coal fields in the Ruhr and iron mines in Lorraine, Germany and France should make no claims on the resources nature gave to us. The argument is still current.

Losses of fishermen at sea have unfortunately continued throughout the 1970s. There were such incidents as the loss of the *St Ibar,* the loss overboard off Clogherhead of an Achill fisherman in the *Wavecrest* in 1971, and now the first of two catastrophes off the Donegal coast, when the *Evelyn Marie* was lost with all hands.

There were 318 men employed in BIM's boatyard in 1975 (76 more than the year before, 219 more than in 1968). Eight new boats over 50 feet long from these yards joined the fleet during the year, and there were eight from other Irish yards and two from abroad. The government undertook to invest £½ million in shellfish farming in Galway bay, an indication that the authorities were cautiously beginning to consider the advantages of fish farming. A new fish cannery was promised for Dungloe and a big complex, now in the final stages of construction, was begun at Castletownbere, to include a factory, freezing plant and cold store. The development of the harbour there was slowly proceeding. During this year also, in spite of strong feelings about the EEC in the industry, it had to be admitted that the operation of the Community's withdrawal price for otherwise unsaleable catches, and of its grant scheme for the Agricultural Guidance and Guarantee Fund (FEOGA) was very helpful to fishermen.

Professor Keady of UCG, speaking in August at the Merriman Summer School, once more clearly and sharply raised the question of fish farming. He demanded the creation of a 'national hatchery' and made a powerful plea for the establishment of shellfisheries in suitable areas where none existed. Meanwhile, UCG, backed by the Maritime Institute, was pressing its long-standing request for the provision of a vessel for basic oceanographic research. This plea was at last accepted and the Oceanography Department now has a (too small) research vessel at its disposal.

George Morrison's prize-winning docu-

Fish processing plant, Cahirciveen

mentary film *Look to the Sea* was put
on show for the first time in October
1975, as part of BIM's programme
to educate the public, and above all
young people, about the history and
the value of our fishing industry.

In November 1975 a formidable
document was submitted to the government jointly by the Irish Fishermen's
Organisation, the Irish Federation of
Marine Industries, the Irish Fish Processors' and Exporters' Association and
the Retail Fish Merchants' Association;
it was called *An Overall Fisheries
Development Plan*. Among its many
suggestions was one that BIM should
be reorganized to consist of a board of

ten instead of six as at present, seven
of the ten to be elected representatives
in varying proportions of the four
bodies submitting the proposals. It was
urged that the reorganised BIM be given
more extensive powers similar to those
exercised in Britain by the White Fish
Authority, which were detailed. It was
suggested that a representative con-
sultative body be set up by the
government to advise about pollution;
that a second training college be
established in the southern half of the
country; that the state acquire a fully
equipped middle-water boat to act both
as a fishery training vessel and a research
ship; that existing research be coordinat-

ed and expanded under a single direction with more consultation with fishermen about the type of fishery exploration needed; that advisory services be made available at all levels in the industry as has been done for agriculture; that an educational drive be launched as a matter of urgency through the Irish Agricultural Organisation Society to improve the operation of fishermen's co-operatives. And there were other proposals about the need for a minister for fisheries, marketing, boat purchase and fishery limits.

An incident in May 1975 raised an uproar among inshore fishermen in Dublin bay, sore ever since Erskine Childers had lifted the very old ban on trawlers fishing between Howth Head and Sorrento Point. A sizeable trawler ran ashore at Blackrock after fouling her screw in her nets just off shore. It is doubtful if sufficient research has been done in Dublin bay, and in a number of other coastal areas, for categorical assertions to be made that they are not breeding grounds, particularly as inshoremen who have always fished there, as their fathers did before, are convinced that they are.

1976 saw a further rise in both landings (tonnage up 6 per cent, value up from £10.5 to £15.3 million), and exports including direct landings abroad which reached £22.6 million. The industry's contribution to gross national pro-

Galway port during the Spring herring season

Bulgarian and Romanian freezer trawlers buying mackerel in Killybegs

duct went up £6.9 million to £33.6 million. A feature of the year was the dramatic fall in herring catches — 24 per cent. The fact that the industry could take this in its stride was a sign of its greatly increased maturity since the dark days fifty years and 100 years earlier when the failure of herring shoals to appear meant disaster for the industry and grim poverty for fishermen. It was takings of sole, haddock, cod, whiting, plaice, sprats and mackerel that covered the deficiency of herrings. The catch by drift net salmon fishermen that year added a further £3.7 million to the value of the total catch.

During 1976 the long drawn-out controversy about the future of our salmon fisheries grew in intensity. Since 1964 the number of salmon dying from a disease called ulcerative dermal necrosis had grown alarmingly, yet 1975 had seen a record catch of 2100 tons, 72 per cent of it by drift net men against only 28 per cent ten years before. The drift net

men contended that there were more salmon available than were being caught and that it was folly to leave it so; others argued that stocks were being dangerously depleted and that the netsmen, now venturing further out to sea, were catching stocks heading for Scottish and English rivers. The secretary to the Foyle Fisheries Commission, in a speech reported by *The Irish Times* on 28 May that gave rise to a long editorial, said drift net men should have a right rather than require a licence to catch salmon. They should be assured 'an adequate and fair income' while steps must be taken to prevent gross over- or under-exploitation of the resource. Amidst a welter of arguments that continue to the time of writing certain realities began to appear. Catches were falling off. Salmon was regaining its traditional status as a food for the people and no longer to be regarded, as it had been for a century and a half, as a luxury to be caught and consumed only by the rich. Drift net men had a right to a decent living in return for exercise of their skills and for the risks they ran. But conservation, inspection and more research were crying necessities, which could not however be adequately met without co-operation and consultation with the net men.

In 1976 the Northern fisheries had a record year. The 290 boats employed landed 15,579 tons in the North and 8,004 tons outside it — a total value of £4,246,128, no less than 49 per cent above 1975's record catch. It was estimated that there were three jobs on shore now in processing, marketing, and ancillary trades and occupations, for every man fishing at sea, a distinctly higher proportion than we have achieved. The value added to fish when processed ashore was calculated as more than 100 per cent. A Northern Ireland Fish Producers' Organisation was set up with more than a third of the boats fishing already involved, and making maximum use of the EEC compensation arrangements for fish withdrawn from human consumption for use as fish meal, silage or pet food. Northern Ireland has an intelligently structured Fishery Harbour Authority, consisting of two elected fishermen, two processors and two members appointed officially. During the year it carried out big improvements at Kilkeel and smaller ones at Ardglass, and began providing ice-making facilities at Ardglass and Portavogie.

Big progress occurred in Ireland in 1976 in takings of oysters, prawns and crabs and in the development of mussel farming in Wexford harbour. There was a large increase in investment in the processing industry ashore. Sixteen new vessels over 50 feet long, five of them over 80 feet long, were added to the fleet; they were worth nearly £5 million in all and fourteen of them were built in Ireland. Sixteen further

such vessels were on order, including eight built in steel. Forty new boats under 50 feet long joined the fleet. Human consumption of fish reached a new high level of 11.6 lbs per head.

It was in 1976 that BIM won international recognition on a high level by securing the PA-Vision European Management Award for the excellence of its relations with the community at large, its persistent efforts to bring constructive relief to depressed areas, its contribution to ecological awareness and its fight against pollution. The event was signalised by publication of a centre-spread article in the Bulletin of the Department of Foreign Affairs.

Throughout 1976 the battle to try to obtain an exclusive, Irish 50-mile zone was waged. The need for it seemed to be re-emphasised by the frequent encroachment of foreign trawlers into our waters. Soviet, Bulgarian and Romanian skippers of large fishing vessels were convicted in Cork for fishing inside our internationally accepted limits, and trawlers from a number of other nations were observed, and some intercepted, by Naval Service ships. The crisis over the desired 50-mile zone led Michael O'Kennedy, soon to become Minister of Foreign Affairs, to declare that the EEC had no right to impose a 200-mile economic zone around the member states and that this state should make a unilateral claim to such a zone for itself. County councils, Workers' Union of Ireland members employed by BIM, trade union branches, Waterford Harbour Board and numerous individuals in letters to the press and in newspaper articles expressed demands to Brussels for recognition of Ireland's right to the exclusive 50-mile zone. Discussions were dragging on in Brussels with the responsible EEC Commissioner and his staff; the 50-mile exclusive zone

Kilkeel, the leading Northern Ireland fishing port

was in the end proclaimed unilaterally, but temporarily, by the government of the day.

Most active of all in pushing the demand were the fishermen themselves, backed by the Irish Fish Producers' Organisation, a recently established body representative of all sections of the industry and recognised by the EEC. The Irish Fishermen's Organisation organised a successful petition on the subject, sent representatives to argue in Brussels, and stirred Irish-American personalities to try to enlist the support of the President of the United States. In the autumn one of the most remarkable gatherings Dublin has ever witnessed took place in the Mansion House. Spokesmen from each of the political parties, the Irish Congress of Trade Unions, leading individual unions, the Maritime Institute, women's, youth and cultural societies, and of course the fishermen themselves, presided over by the Lord Mayor of the capital, verbally pledged support for the 50-mile demand and signed a pledge to keep up the battle. A short-lived but temporarily very active body was elected by this mass meeting to plan a long range campaign for the conservation of our fishing communities.

Meanwhile another and very significant event had occurred which is bound to exercise increasing influence on the industry's future. This was the entry of the Irish Transport and General Workers' Union (ITGWU) in a serious way into the business of organising trawler deckhands. The industry had now grown large enough for a variety of different interests to emerge. The Irish Fishermen's Organisation could speak with authority, and continuously did and does so, on behalf of the skippers of larger boats. But it could not adequately represent

On deck

the interests of the small inshore men, who have indeed taken steps only a few months before the writing of these words to build their own national organisation. Nor could it express, now that trawlers were so much bigger and dearer (Ireland would soon be seeing its first £1 million trawler), the aspirations of deck-hands who, however great their skills, could never in existing circumstances hope to become large-trawler skippers themselves.

The public first became aware of the growth of the union organisation of deck-hands when disputes occurred in the autumn of 1976 in Howth and Skerries. Those closely concerned with the industry realised what an important new factor had come into play when they received from the National Fishermen's Branch of the ITGWU a closely reasoned statement on the meeting of EEC foreign ministers at The Hague on 30 October when Ireland's unilateral claim was inserted in the minutes. The statement maintained, correctly as it turned out, that this gesture had no legal validity since we had irrevocably accepted the conditions of EEC membership. It demanded precise clarification of assertions made by the Minister for Foreign Affairs and by BIM that in the next few years we would be adding 300 vessels to our fleet and doubling our catch. It concluded by declaring that such gestures as putting forward a unilateral claim to a 50-mile zone were only playing to the gallery in the absence of a fully thought-out national fishery policy designed to enable Irish vessels to exploit effectively the 50-mile zone, Irish experts to conserve and manage the zone, and Irish processors to handle the increased catch.

The National Fishermen's Branch of the Union followed this statement up a few weeks later with a memorandum to the Minister for Fisheries on EEC fishery policy. It began by demanding the implementation of an effective policy of conservation of fish stocks, based on a system of fishing zones according to the size of the vessel fishing. It rejected any system of national fish catch quotas founded on average past catches — this discriminated in favour of countries with long established fishing industries and against Ireland with an industry only in the process of development. It pointed out that Britain and Ireland were being asked to police 80 per cent of the waters claimed by the EEC largely for the benefit of their continental partners. The Branch made it clear that it was demanding democratic control of the exploitation of the country's resources in fish, negotiations at national level involving all parties directly concerned in the catching of fish about future operation of the 'share' system, a guaranteed basic minimum earning for all engaged in catching and a comprehensive insurance scheme that would take into account the special hazards facing fishermen.

An article in *The Irish Times* on 3 October 1976 on the deadlock in Brussels on the 50-mile limit question sadly but correctly assessed the situation: 'Considering the way Ireland has so grossly neglected the wealth of its fish resources and even now after a decade of expansion only manages to catch 10 per cent of the fish netted in Irish waters it is difficult to see how the EEC Commission could have been much more understanding'. Refusal of an exclusive 50-mile zone was disappointing but, considering that special treatment was being offered instead, less bad than some headlines suggested.

The Irish Times article turned out to be reasonably correct in the end. Fifteen months later under a new government a complicated zoning system began to be worked out which did indeed ensure protection for our inshore fishermen. Larger boats further out are subject to competition which will get fiercer when Spain's big fishing fleet has free access to the 200-mile belt on that country's entry into the EEC. (Spanish trawlers in the late 1970s seemed even to be courting arrest by prematurely fishing in these waters, perhaps in order to establish a case for special rights based on custom.)

1976, therefore, was an eventful year. And to add to public concern about the industry there were headlines in November about under-sized oysters being dredged in Kerry and headlines in October about mackerel being dumped back into the sea, though housewives were paying 30p a pound for them, because processing plants in Donegal and the Mornington fishmeal factory could not handle them. Then, in the last week in November, the Burtonport trawler *Carrig Una* was lost with all hands near where the *Evelyn Marie* had been wrecked less than two years earlier — a desperate blow to a small community intimately connected with fishing and the sea. *The Irish Times* wrote: 'Ted Carbery, the skipper of the wrecked trawler *Carrig Una*, like his brother Denis, was among the modern young fishermen now commanding vessels in the growing Irish fishing fleet. He took his Second Hand Special examination and passed, which is the necessary qualification to take charge of a 65 foot trawler. If he had been a Norwegian or an Icelander, a Frenchman or a Pole, his training standards would have been very much higher, and the contingencies which can be unexpectedly met at sea could be tackled with knowledge gained from other people's experience. But that was not the case, because this country still fails to give its fishermen a level of training equal to the responsibilities

or the rewards.' It was not in fact until 1979 that BIM was at last granted sole control of the training of fishermen and immediately made it clear that before long no skipper will be allowed to acquire a trawler of 65 feet or more unless he holds a skipper's certificate of competency.

The industry entered 1977, therefore, not only in mourning but faced with a series of internal and external problems demanding better educational and training standards and the restructuring of the industry so as to secure the maximum unity of all sectors in the face of dangers and opportunities.

There were now nearly 2,300 full-time fishermen and more than 4,000 fishing part-time (and it has to be remembered that even sea-fishing is becoming less labour-intensive with the growing sophistication of equipment). They landed £18.7 million worth of fish in home ports during 1977, 45 per cent more in value than the year before, and £2.1 million worth in ports outside the state. The tonnage landed in ports in the state was up 2 per cent. Exports at £27.49 million were up nearly £5 million and the industry's contribution to the gross national product went up by £14.9 million. There were big increases in takings of mackerel and Dublin Bay prawns.

Throughout the year the struggle continued to try to secure the 50-mile exclusive zone. Ministers were obviously influenced by the intensity of the feelings expressed and the cogency of the arguments advanced in favour of Irish exploitation of what the public now saw as an Irish natural resource. In particular, they saw the deficiencies of the quota systems proposed in Brussels. Who was going to supervise to see no trawler exceeded its quota? (Months later the Irish Fishermen's Organisation promulgated a plan for the planting of inspectors

Fishermen protesting in Dublin during the campaign for the 50 mile exclusive fishing limit

in each boat fishing within fifty miles of Ireland.) The country was virtually promised that there would be no backing down on the 50-mile demand. But by the end of the year it was evident that forces had built up which were making it impossible for the Irish government to hold out. Moreover the industry itself was suffering from loss of investment and a decline in morale owing to continuing uncertainty.

Towards the end of the year Brian Lenihan accepted an interim zoning plan, and the two-day fishermen's strike and the Dublin demonstration in February 1978, coinciding as they did with the ruling of the European Court that the previous government's exclusion of large foreign trawlers from the 50-mile limit was invalid, marked the conclusion of this lengthy battle. If the battle itself was lost, the Irish people's interest in the fishing industry had been won and so at last had the authorities' realisation that our fisheries would no longer afford to be neglected. *The Irish Times* wrote in an editorial on 17 February 1978: 'Yet there is hope on the horizon, even

for young trawler skippers with £300,000 boats to pay off. Europe's shrinking fishing fleets have few grounds left to them to make up a year's economic working, so that the run down of their fleets which is rapidly taking place is in Ireland's interest.'

That the future will lie in the end with fish farming was fortunately an idea that continued to gain ground. An informed *Irish Times* article in October 1977 pointed out that whereas fish farming in Italy was producing 17,000 tons of edible fish a year, 15,000 in Denmark, 13,000 in France (France hopes by the 1990s to be farm-producing all the 15,000 tons of salmon it consumes), and even 450 in Switzerland, our fish farm production was only 170 tons. The enormous possibilities, however, were clearly spelled out.

There was good news on the progress of mussel production under the auspices of Gaeltarra Eireann in the west of Ireland. Clarenbridge Oyster Co-Operative, with over sixty members, was asserting that within four years its business should be worth £2 million

Oyster dredging, Clarinbridge, Co. Galway

Oyster spatting ponds in the upper reaches of Cork Harbour

a year, and was preparing for bigger export orders than ever from Denmark, the Netherlands and Germany. The number of licences for drift netting for salmon was not reduced.

The Irish Fishermen's Organisation added to its 50-mile demand another demand for a sworn enquiry into the cost of fishing boats in Ireland, alleging that an Irish-built vessel could cost £200,000 more than a similar one built abroad.

It was calculated that if a five-man trawler operating out of Howth caught £200 worth of fish in a day, £60 would go for running expenses, £70 to the skipper as owner, £14 to him as crew member and £14 each to the other four. Some believe that this traditional

share out scheme is the best suited still for the industry but not all. The future will no doubt see disputes, but if it is also to see the progress of the last seventeen years culminate in the acceptance by Europe of Ireland as a principal fish producer there is going to have to be the closest co-operation and the most open consultation between skippers, deck-hands, BIM, the scientists and the state authorities.

The Northern Ireland fisheries far surpassed even their 1976 record. They landed nearly 28,000 tons of fish at a value of £7.15 million, up 59 per cent. There was a big increase in the cod catch, and a ready market was being found for squid, landings of which had risen from nil a few years back to 230

Howth before undergoing major reconstruction 1980

metric tons. The number of full-time fish-processing firms had now risen to twenty-five, and a start had been made on the major redevelopment of Portavogie at an estimated ultimate cost of £3.8 million. Enforcement of conservation measures for herring in the Manx and Mourne areas, drawn up in concert with the EEC, was strict.

1978 here can perhaps best be described as a year of expectation. There was a 23 per cent increase in the value of landings and a 19 per cent increase in volume up to what forty years ago would have seemed the totally unattainable figure of 98,000 metric tons. Pelagic landings largely mackerel accounted for the increase.

Legislation was introduced to permit the imposition of much heavier penalties on foreign poachers in our waters. The need for this was made more clear than ever when Dutch trawler skippers won an appeal against gear-confiscation on the grounds that it had been unconstitutional. The Dutch and Irish governments reached an agreement about fishing rights off our west coast which proved only partly satisfactory in practice. Several more Spanish trawlers were arrested before an agreement made with the Spaniards, who were negotiating EEC entry, barred them temporarily from coming within fifty miles of Ireland. Irish trawlers defied the EEC ban on herring fishing in the Celtic Sea (and were reprimanded by the *Skipper*), and the Naval Service had a clash with alleged illegal drift net fishermen. There was also a local 'oyster war' in Kerry. All these incidents were basically part of the malaise afflicting the industry, and still afflicting it at the time of writing, in the continued absence of a detailed, constructive EEC fishery policy within which BIM and the fishermen's organi-

Killybegs today. Though this is our major fishing port, the facilities available are not sufficiently adequate

sations could plan the future of our own industry.

There were still, however, many positive signs of health in the industry besides its quantitative growth. This was well illustrated in a very attractive leaflet published by BIM to convince young people of the wisdom of making fishing a career. 1978 incidentally was the year when for the first time women were to be found working at sea in our fishing fleet — another sign of its growing maturity. The BIM leaflet pointed out that there were now 8,000 people working full-time or part-time in a fleet of more than 2,700 vessels, and emphasised not only the breadth of knowledge required to succeed in sea fishing today but also the rewards, psychological as well as financial, and the comforts as well as the gadgetry in one of our larger trawlers.

In June 1978 Brian Lenihan opened a long-needed Fisheries Research Centre at Abbotstown, County Dublin which has attracted a keen and conscientious staff. This evidence of an understanding in high quarters, however belated, of the paramount necessity for more and more research if our industry is to prosper in the new conditions arising was warmly welcomed by all concerned. It justified the innumerable articles in the *Skipper*, demands by the Maritime Institute, promptings by experts at UCG and elsewhere, which had aired the case for more research for more than thirty years. Moreover, it was in 1978 that a new, larger and better equipped fishery research vessel was promised to replace the *Cu Feasa* and *Cu na Mara,* recently discarded as obsolete. Meanwhile the former fishing vessel the 69 foot *Lough Beltra* was commissioned by the National Board of Science and Technology as a research craft available to state bodies, universities and other interested concerns for time-charter

research projects.

In July 1978 the *Skipper* reported a development reflecting the new dimension which had entered the industry with the establishment of the Fishermen's Branch of the ITGWU. The Branch was demanding that the reconstruction of Howth harbour should include the provision of a social centre for deckhands, including shower-rooms and wash-rooms, a hall for functions, table-tennis facilities and so on. The paper endorsed this demand as entirely reasonable and put forward suggestions about how it could be implemented.

In September 1978 an arrangement was made with the EEC for 50 per cent grants through BIM for new boats from 6 metres upwards. This meant that the inshore fishermen could now begin re-equipping their fleet, and the news was hailed with gratitude by the new National Salmon and Inshore Fishermen's Association, set up earlier in the year.

Other good news was the successful revival after forty years of the drift net herring fishery at Downings, County Donegal, where up to twenty-four half-deckers and several craft in the 45 foot to 52 foot class from various adjacent parts of Donegal had based themselves. The European demand for herring had put the price up to nearly £20 a box, but as the *Skipper* wrote, these boats, normally fishing with six men for fifteen hours on end through the night in open North Atlantic conditions, deserved every pound they earned.

After a long period of suspicion and argument, moreover, the fishermen of West Cork came around to accepting that the establishment of a big Spanish processing factory at Castletownbere, to be fed by Irish and Spanish fishermen in co-operation, would be greatly to their advantage. The initial arrangement was

Foreign trawlers lying up in Dublin in the late 1970s

for three Spanish trawlers to be registered in Ireland, taking on partly Irish crews,

Finally, news came in December 1978 that testified to the confidence which the recent history of the industry had generated, and enormously heartened and deeply touched all who took in its significance. It was a personal gesture towards the industry by somebody whose name in seventeen years had grown to be synonymous with Irish sea fishing. Brendan O'Kelly, chairman and chief executive of BIM, had been invited in 1976 to distant Tasmania to advise the state government how to make something of a hitherto sadly neglected fishing industry. He had produced a 50-page blueprint full of practical suggestions which resulted in the establishment of the Tasmanian Fisheries Development Authority. During 1978 he had gone back for a three-month spell as the Authority's first Chairman. Once again his drive and expertise delighted everyone and one newspaper wrote that his work was 'the biggest and best thing that has happened to

fishing in the state, and possibly Australia'. Others were equally full of praise. The Tasmanian government took the hint and asked Brendan O'Kelly to take for five years not only the chairmanship of the Fisheries Authority but also of a wide-ranging resources development council. He was to get £30,000 a year and a free house — more than double what BIM gives him. Brendan O'Kelly preferred to stay with BIM in Ireland. (One Killybegs skipper has recently been known to earn more in a month than Tasmania was offering for a year to Brendan O'Kelly, whose salary here is surpassed by some Killybegs deck-hands.)

1979 began with an announcement on 4 January of the greatest significance for the industry's future. BIM was henceforth to have sole responsibility for the training of fishermen at all levels. The role of the National Fisheries Training Centre at Greencastle was being enlarged to provide external courses, including a mobile training unit, and a training vessel, so sadly lacking hitherto, was to be provided for giving instruction in fishing techniques, navigation and safety. Training for existing fishermen was to be given top priority through expansion of already established BIM port courses. New recruits were to be given a two to four weeks' introductory sea trip, followed by six to eight weeks at Greencastle. They would then receive a fisherman's discharge book and service record. They would next go back to sea for a minimum of six months as 'deckie learner'. After that there were eight weeks' more advanced training at Greencastle, followed by an oral and written examination to be passed before obtaining the BIM Deckhand Certificate.

Training will be tightened up and improved right up the scale, with 90 per cent attendance at all courses obligatory, and from Janaury 1983 no skipper will receive a new vessel under BIM's schemes unless he has the necessary qualifying certificate. In an age when fishing vessels are costing up to £1 million and are full of complicated electronic equipment, when competition from well-trained foreign fishermen is acute and lives are still being lost unnecessarily, these changes are triply welcome.

Later in January 1979 the public learnt that BIM had two trawlers, *Orion* and *Johnny Ruth*, on charter and operating from Rossaveal to survey for undiscovered sources of fish along

Trainee fishermen leave for the Greencastle Fishery Training Centre to start on a three-month full time induction course in fisheries training (February 1980) Included are: Terence Byrne, Artane, Dublin; Seamus Larkin, Arklow; Patrick Curran, Newry; Brian Treanor, Newry; Gabriel Hesnan, Navan; Mark Molloy, Sutton, Co. Dublin; Thomas Matthews, Drumree, Co. Meath; Paul O'Reilly and Peter O'Keefe Blackrock, Co. Dublin; Michael Barrett, Lettermullen, Co. Galway; Joseph Pender, Ennis; David Murphy, Ballina; Martin Duffy, Westport; John Wilkes, Ballina; Seán Ó Gúairim, Carna, Co. Galway; Martin Attridge, Schull, Co. Cork; John Corbett, Janesboro, Co. Limerick; Peter Mackey, Tralee; Ken O'Neill, Dunmore East; Brendan Holland, Cork; Ronnie Smith, Bantry; John Tangney, Castlemaine, Co. Kerry

the west coast. Very large concentrations of mackerel were found and also further out to sea, horse-mackerel which is a coarser variety of mackerel much prized in parts of Africa and Eastern Europe. Horse mackerel is already being exported from Cahirciveen to destinations in Africa. It was aboard these vessels that women crew members shipped for the first time. At the same time BIM reported success in the exploitation of blue whiting in the Porcupine Bank area west of Galway. This fish is now being caught, processed and exported in fair quantities. A Northern Ireland trawler, the *Green Isle II* of Kilkeel, had been on charter to the British White Fish Authority to catch blue whiting for a market research programme.

The disaster that destroyed the French tanker *Betelgeuse* in Bantry bay in January 1979 led once again to pollution of local fishing areas, affected by previous spills at the Whiddy Island, Gulf Oil terminal, and raised the question of who was to pay compensation.

A white paper on the country's economic prospects promised publication of a detailed study by the Economic and Social Research Institute which should act as foundation for further state activity to foster the industry, and gave encouraging news of progress in research for an operation of mariculture projects, some of which seemed on the verge of achieving full commercial production. A parliamentary bill was also introduced aiming at the revival of our salmon fisheries which were worth, according to Brian Lenihan, £5 million annually in exports and £15 million to tourism.

The salmon crisis was the occasion of a useful and well-attended meeting at the Royal Dublin Society sponsored by the journal *Rod and Gun* for the Institute of Fisheries Management. The chief inspector of the Northumbrian Water Authority in north-east England outlined the problems experienced there and the methods used to combat poaching, illegal net meshes and other violations of conservation regulations. It was agreed that with our long coastline we had particular difficulties to overcome, that the various governments concerned should get together and work out a uniform plan for salmon conservation, and that there should be more co-operation and consultation among all concerned at home. In July 1979 the National Salmon and Inshore Fishermen's Association produced a widely publicised book entitled *Irish Salmon, A Future?*, at the launching of which Brian Lenihan was present. The Association demanded quick measures to reduce pollution and other physical threats to salmon, a vast national hatchery policy and a long-term fishery policy. The Minister expressed optimism about the stock situation, promised a hatchery programme, insisted that drift net men were no danger to the salmon industry provided they kept to the regulations, and spoke of that well-rooted Irish phenomenon 'too much invested dissension' among people involved in salmon fishing.

Problems remained in other branches of the industry. The processors complained that the factories were working seriously under capacity. White fish landed met the demands of the home market with only a small surplus most of which was exported fresh. An EEC expert declared that fresh fish consumption was declining in Western Europe generally but consumption of processed and frozen fish was going up. A British expert who had carried out an extensive survey of radio-active contamination of fish in the Irish Sea by the Windscale nuclear power plant in Cumbria asserted

An ancillary industry — net-making and repair in Howth

that fresh fish was the safest food product on the market.

BIM, starved of the capital needed to convert its boatyards at Dingle, Baltimore and Killybegs to construction of modern steel trawlers, was faced with the choice of closing them or trying to sell them to private enterprise. This caused a flurry of very understandable protests and vain deputations to see the Minister. Some 300 workers earning £70 to £80 a week were involved; in the case of Baltimore the livelihood of the whole community was threatened and the expected emigration of the work force led to fear that the famous Baltimore lifeboat station would have to close for lack of crewmen. At the time of writing, in fact, private concerns have taken over the Baltimore, Killybegs and Dingle yards. The *Skipper* commented on the boatyards crisis as follows:

The decision will not cause any fewer boats to be built, but it does mean that the orders will go to the yards of private concerns which have been more efficient in their utilisation of manpower. BIM's administration cannot be blamed for this, for the State's rôle as an employer never takes into consideration the productivity norms which private enterprise must observe.

Apart from pressures on the Government from the private builders there is a deeper reason why the decision was taken. If enlightened leadership had been given to the training efforts of the Department over the past three years, there would be plenty of young fishermen coming forward today to fill every shipyard berth we have. But that has not been the case, hence the lack of work to

The Father Murphy, Ireland's first steel-hulled trawler, built in Poland, 80 feet

keep all yards busy.

In the interests of the future, with the bitter experience of hardship to boatwrights' families, let everybody in the industry now play their part to rectify this serious mistake. BIM's fundamental purpose is to develop and promote the industry, and belately it has just been given the task of re-organising fishermen's training. Now let us build on a stronger foundation: our fish resources have never been more valuable.

There arose also the problem of conservation of mackerel stock, now that this fish had taken the herring's place as the principal catch for large sections of our fleet. A big influx of Dutch trawlers catching mackerel was noted.

However, there was much in 1979 to encourage hopes that the industry would accomplish the task of making itself in due course the most important fishing industry in Western Europe. The Irish Fishermen's Organisation made a significant gesture towards the deckhands. It condemned trawler skippers who refused to give crews full financial details of catches, thus preventing them checking the share received against the value of the catch. 'It is unjust,' said Joey Murrin, chairman of the Irish Fishermen's Organisation, 'for any fisherman to be deprived of the right to check his earnings against the earnings and expenses of the vessel.'

Kinsale Vocational School, having thoroughly established its marine course, acquired a 26 foot long folkboat yacht, *Solveig,* as a training vessel. The pupils would not only train aboard during the summer, but overhaul the *Solveig* and make any necessary repairs during the winter months. Tom Geoghegan, market development manager at BIM, told readers of the *Skipper* that he was very hopeful about the future of the processing industry, emphasising the particular successes of a recently set up plant at Dungloe, with big orders for canned mackerel and herring, the big prospects for the Spanish-Irish project at Castletownbere, especially in processing hake 'hitherto not landed in any sizeable volume in this country' (since Renaissance times, he should have said as we have seen), the spectacular success of a Wexford firm in winning continental export markets, especially for a retail pack of mussel meat in the half shell for France, and a new shellfish plant at Balbriggan.

A boy, Michael Kett of Ennis, won the National Fish Cookery Contest, another piece of news inconceivable a few years ago and surely proof of the spread of the pleasure and above all the possibility of eating fish throughout the country.

The loss of three Achill Island fishermen and their boat *Lios Carra* early in July 1979 off Dooega Head was one more reminder of the dangers of the fishermen's life and the absolute necessity for every possible step to be taken, ashore and afloat, to minimise those dangers. Only a few weeks later an Aran trawlerman lost his life loading goods on a fishing craft in Galway.

In May 1979 the Irish Fishermen's Organisation held a ceremony which

The Fish Cookery Centre, run by BIM, in Dublin

holds much hope for the future, at BIM's Fish Cookery Centre in Dublin. This was when Joey Murrin, the organisation's energetic and far-seeing chairman, at the core of all the controversies in which the industry has been engaged since 1975, announced that his organisation would issue awards twice annually for the three best trainees emerging from the Greencastle course examinations. He said that the fishermen of the future would have to embrace a combination of both old and new and have the skills of his predecessors joined to expertise in modern technology.

A few weeks later Joey Murrin, who had become a figure nearly as familiar to the Irish public as Brendan O'Kelly, reached the end of his four year spell as chairman of the Irish Fishermen's Organisation and handed over to the very capable Brian Crummey. Interviewed by Radio Telefís Éireann on this occasion, Joey Murrin expressed confidence in the industry's future in spite of the failure to win the 50-mile limit with which he had come to be associated. He thought politicians who promised to keep up the fight for the limit had never really believed it was achievable, but for their own purposes had led the public to believe it was. He had been naive enough to think it was, but at least the fight for it had united the industry, and the public behind it, and shown the power and value of such unity. Ireland being where she is on the edge of Europe's finest fishing grounds seems naturally destined to become the centre of the western European fishing industry, and the growing cost and scarcity of fuel on the continent should help even more to make it so. It was up to us to exploit these advantages to the full.

Down the centuries the Irish sea fishing industry has moved from a position of pride and prosperity before the seventeenth century, through a series of prolonged crises and brief revivals, to a point where, after a steady period of real growth, the public has become aware of its importance and its leading figures have become personalities always in the public eye.

9

Looking to the Future

We are an island people that has produced some of the finest seamen, scientists and inventors who have participated in man's age old struggle to understand better and make wiser use of the element that makes up 71 per cent of the globe he lives in.

Countless Irishmen have been lost at sea in a vast variety of disasters, many of them sea fishermen. Now as a nation we face, inside the European Community and as a member of the greater world community of the United Nations, not only new difficulties but also new opportunities. Part of the task of surmounting the difficulties and seizing the opportunities can be accomplished by carefully developing the fishing industry, which has at last shown its ability to achieve the successes believed possible by thinking people for three and a half centuries but made impossible by ill-will or ignorance in high places.

A prosperous Irish fishing industry will not only give increasing employment ashore and afloat — all of it, with the advance of technology in all fields, potentially interesting and stimulating as well as remunerative — but it will also provide more food in greater variety at home, and enable Ireland to play a fuller part in feeding a hungry world.

But to attain a state of permanent prosperity the industry, as we have seen, has still to journey far, imaginatively and courageously. If, as some have predicted, we are to reach a catch worth £800 million a year — think what an injection that would be into the Irish economy — it is clear that the industry will have to overcome its internal contradictions and climb upward to a situation where research and planning and the highest standards of education and training will be considered as indispensable as, recently, they appeared unattainable. This will require sustained public support, which the industry will continue to have to earn by its own successes. It will require political intelligence at the top, not only to assist planning and finance research but also to show our European partners that Ireland, having acquired a buoyant fishing industry of its own, is the natural centre for fishing and fish-processing for all of western Europe. Ireland could supply both its own needs and an export market which sane and enlightened international trade policies should help to grow indefinitely. And if Ireland does become western Europe's fishing centre, Irish fishermen have a right to demand that a large share of the catching be left to them provided they continually improve productivity, as the County Down fishermen have so conspicuously proved possible.

Joey Murrin was correct, in his farewell interview as chairman of the Irish

Joey Murrin, chairman of the Irish Fishermen's Organisation

Fishermen's Organisation, to show sympathy for the British fishermen objecting to their continental partners wanting unlimited rights in traditional British waters. We have a common cause with the British in this respect, but the other EEC nations, further from the fishing grounds and so more heavily handicapped by fuel costs and scarcities, have a common cause with both of us in the need to create the most flourishing fishing industry possible where it is economically most sensible to create it, as close as possible to the fishing grounds. Finn Gundelach, Vice-President of the Commission of the European Communities, not the Irish fishing industry's best loved European, did say nevertheless at Letterkenny on 17 February, 1978:

It is fair and reasonable, as the Commission has proposed, to reserve especially favourable treatment for the Irish fishing industry within Community policies and it is equally fair and reasonable to suggest that other Community fishermen, in whose markets and for whose assistance in other ways Ireland rightly claims equal treatment as a matter of Community law and solidarity, should continue to fish within strictly controlled limits in waters which have just recently come into Irish fisheries jurisdiction. Any other approach by the Commission would have been one-sided and unjust.

If our industry is to flourish, all involved must be helped to feel equally involved in its success, and this means above all that the ordinary fisherman must feel that his career is worth while, with permanent prospects. The French fishing industry, for instance, which has incidentally no fewer than twenty-eight fishery training schools behind it, provides the ordinary fisherman with an elaborate insurance scheme, quite generous pensions at the age of fifty after twenty-five years' service, and such safeguards as guaranteed proper hours and reasonable duration for meals and guarantees of good quality food on board. Facilities like these, and more care not only over the more dramatic aspects of sea safety but over training in first aid and swimming, must all become commonplace for Irish sea fishermen in the near future.

As has so often been stated in these pages, the future production of fish for eating and eventually perhaps also for fertiliser and cattle-feeding, depends on rapid progress in fish-farming or mariculture; a real breakthrough in this field seems fairly close in Ireland. Whatever economies governments feel they must make, economies in that domain must not be permitted; the future of a large part of mankind, and certainly the future of large areas of the west of Ireland, can be assured by rapid advances in mariculture. Experts in Ireland who were sceptical only a few years ago are now preaching this message. It should not be forgotten, moreover, that the Soviet Union, one of the world's chief landers of fish, expects that by the end of the century it will be producing more fish from farms than by the traditional method of hunting from ships at sea. Japan, another leading fishing nation, is making huge strides in the development of mariculture and is likely to emulate the Soviet Union.

Since 1979 the industry has been in stormy waters. This is largely because the EEC has still not worked out a genuinely cooperative fishery policy. This failure has weakened confidence at home in the continuing growth of the industry and slowed private invest-

ment in it, just when other factors are providing an excuse for cutting investment by the state — a short-sighted reaction which will retard progress that sound policy combined with our unique geographic position ought to guarantee. In the absence, too, of an agreed EEC policy carried out in a disciplined manner there is continued poaching in Irish waters by foreign fishing vessels. The approaching entry of Spain into the EEC seems to be the reason for a continuing series of intrusions by Spanish trawlers into the EEC zone off Ireland's west coast, presumably to try to reinforce a Spanish claim for 'traditional' rights to fish in the area. All this, however, is temporary trouble. There are good signs as well, which include the launching at Castletownbere in April 1981 of the Eiranova complex, a joint Spanish-Irish venture which promises increased employment in the area and a revival of

The £1 million fish processing plant of Eiranova Fisheries Ltd. at Castletownbere, Co. Cork

Three of the most modern purser-trawlers in the Irish fishing fleet — each 133 feet long and costing £2 million. Built in Norway and Holland

the old hake fishery off our south coast. New large trawlers joined the Killybegs fleet in 1980 in spite of rising fuel prices, against which the fishermen have raised a justifiable demand for a fuel subsidy, and dumping of fish in EEC countries from developed non-member states which ought to have been prevented.

There have been calls for the re-organisation and even the abolition of BIM, especially since Brendan O'Kelly resigned at the beginning of 1981. But the most sensible step would probably be to strengthen that organisation and give it undivided responsibility for developing and implementing an Irish national fishery policy as part — and a decisive part — of the ultimately inevitable EEC policy. The need for constant improvement in training for fishermen

and for increased and coordinated research are greater than ever. So, as Mr Paddy Power, Mr Lenihan's successor as Minister for Fisheries, said at a Dublin seminar on fish biology on April 23, 1981, is the responsibility to conserve fish stocks in our waters. Here again, the value of a powerful single body to draw up a fishery policy and get it carried out is clearly indicated.

In 1980, the national catch of 145,000 tonnes, worth £35.6 million, topped all previous records. There is no good reason why this catch, nearly double that of five years earlier, should not double again by the end of the decade. BIM's estimate of the condition of the industry in the spring of 1981 is printed as an appendix (page 175).

Dr Samuel Smiles, a famous moralist of Victorian England and preacher of the virtues of hard work, visited Ireland in 1883. In a widely-read book which he published the following year, *Men of Invention and Industry*, he devoted a chapter to our country 'and the well-known industry of its people'. In it he said that 'there is no reason to despair of seeing, before many years have elapsed, a large development of the fishing industry of Ireland. We may yet see Galway the Yarmouth, Achill the Grimsby, and Killybegs the Wick of the West'. He spoke more truly than he knew; after a false start in the decade after he wrote, and a subsequent long slump, Irish fishing is mounting steadily towards the heights, and could truly rival that of the neighbouring isle in the next century.

All those generations of Irish fishermen who toiled for scanty reward, ignored or despised by the bulk of the population, and all those thousands who have lost their lives in this most exacting of occupations, deserve that we, with all our newly-won opportunites, should succeed in doing what Dr Smiles believed we could. It is not romantic idealism, of course, but enlightened self-interest that creates co-operation among fishermen and gives prosperity to an industry based on the co-operation of all involved. But for self-interest to be enlightened it requires a touch of idealism as well. These are the qualities our industry needs today as never before, qualities which an encouraging number of those concerned with the industry are showing they possess to the full.

Appendix

The Irish Fishing Industry — growth and potential

The national catch of 145,000 tonnes, in 1980, valued at IR£35.6 million, was a record in the history of the fishing industry. Landings of IR£29 million were made into Irish ports while the balance of IR£6.6 million was registered by Irish vessels landing directly into foreign ports. This achievement on the industry's part, was a positive response to the opportunity afforded it, under the terms of the 1976 Hague Agreement, of Ireland doubling its catch. Despite the problems of closed herring fisheries, quotas, scarcity and cost of energy, and the long-awaited Common Fisheries Policy, landings rose from 75,000 tonnes in 1975, valued at IR£9 million, to the record catch of 1980. Inside a decade the value of Ireland's catch went from IR£3.9 million to IR£35.6 million.

The biggest contribution of last year's catch came from mackerel, which has been increasing dramatically in recent years and which has also benefitted from improved marketing arrangements. The Irish quota for mackerel, which was re-negotiated by the Minister for Fisheries and Forestry, stood at 52,000 tonnes in 1980. In addition, salmon catches by drift-net fishermen amounted to IR£3.2 million.

Shellfish landings in recent years

MFW Olgarry returning to Killybegs harbour fully laden with mackerel

have amounted to approximately 11,000 tonnes annually. In 1980, they were valued at IR£6.2 million. Lobsters, crawfish, prawns, crabs and oysters are among the principal varieties.

In the league table, with other EEC countries, the figure for Ireland's landings, taken as a percentage of Gross Domestic Product, is second only to that of Denmark, a country renowned for its fishing industry.

Markets:

The size of the home market is quite small with a population of just over three million people. The most popular varieties are plaice, whiting, cod and haddock. Domestic consumption of fish has risen from 10.1 lbs. per head per year in 1970 to 11.7 lbs. in 1979, an increase of 16%. This is a substantial achievement in a country in which the eating of fish was until recent times influenced by penitential connotations, and it has been largely brought about by the comprehensive advertising and promotional campaign launched during these years by the industry and BIM. There has also been a major improvement in the distributive pattern of fish over the years with the influence of the Dublin Market declining and more fish being distributed directly from the ports, through fishermen's co-operatives and the trade, to the neighbouring hinterlands.

There has been marked progress in Irish fish exports since 1970. At that time export earnings from domestic landings, including salmon and freshwater fish amounted to IR£3 million and by 1980 they had increased to IR£41 million with a further IR£6.6 million being exported directly by fishing vessels landing at foreign ports. During recent years BIM's policy has been geared towards achieving as much added value

as possible in exports for the expansion of fish processing activities. Up to the seventies there was only a limited quantity of fish processed in any form here, but this has now been improved by the establishment of processing facilities grant-aided by the IDA and Udaras na Gaeltachta. Processing firms with BIM assistance have succeeded in multiplying the value of exports since the early seventies. Over the years the United Kingdom has been and still is, the main export market, taking over 25% of the country's exports. The other principal markets are France, Germany, Netherlands, Belgium and Sweden.

Herring has been by far the greatest single species of fish exported and accounted for something in the region of 50% of total fish exports in every year until 1976. The importance of herring is now declining because of the supply position and a concentrated effort is being successfully made to develop exports of mackerel and other pelagic species as well as placing greater emphasis on demersal fish. Shell-fish account for over 28% and salmon for about 12% of exports. Fish exports account for over 1.5% of total exports from Ireland. Only one other country in the EEC — Denmark — has a higher percentage than this with over 5% while the proportion for the other countries is less than 1%.

Employment:
The number of people employed in all sectors of the industry has risen considerably over the years. Excluding those engaged in distribution total employment between 1970 and 1980 showed a growth of 57% with the number of full-time fishermen increasing by 78% and part-time by 37%. The shore processing employment sector showed an increase of 74%, while

TABLE 1* *Employment in the fishing industry*

	1970	1980	% Increase
Fishermen full-time	1,960	3,485	78%
Fishermen part-time	3,900	5,333	37%
Fishermen total	5,860	8,818	50%
Shore processing	920	1,600	79%
Other full-time employment (excl. distribution)	360	770	114%
Total employment (excl. distribution)	7,140	11,188	57%

*It should be noted that these figures are best estimates.

other full-time employment increased by over 110%. Table 1 gives details of the various sectors.

Actual employment figures in the regions do not reflect fully the total socio-economic benefit of fisheries activity in the different coastal areas. The important measure is the maintenance of the demographic structure in coastal regions through additional employment in the service and ancillary sector of the industry.

Investment — catching sector:

Investment in the fleet has increased substantially over the last 10 years, from IR£5 million to over IR£70 million. Table 2 shows the growth in the number and size of vessels in the fleet:

This shows a trend towards larger vessels which commenced in 1974 and has continued since. In the past year, there has been a move by some of the more progressive fishermen to seek larger more sophisticated type fishing vessels in the size range 110-140 ft in order to tap the potential resources lying further offshore from our coasts. These include species such as blue whiting, mackerel, scad and hake, species which are not yet used commercially as food fish in this country but for which there is likely to be growing demand in export markets in the future. Four such super trawlers, in the 133 ft size range joined the Irish fleet last year and an additional vessel, also in the super trawler class, is ex-

TABLE 2

Vessel length (ft.)	1970	1975	1979	1980
Under 50	1,772	2,006	2,614	2,686
51—65	160	175	148	154
66—72	57	106	109	110
73—90	26	57	89	105
Over 90	—	2	5	9

pected to be operational with the fleet towards the middle of the year. Bigger, faster and better equipped than any boats ever to have worked out of an Irish port, these 133 ft trawlers cost about IR£2 million each and have already extended the important mackerel season by operating in waters outside the range of the present fleet.

Investment — shore industry

Investment in shore-based industry continues to rise and now over fifty seafood processing establishments employ more than 1,600 people. Fixed asset investment in this sector has risen from less than IR£2 million to about IR£16 million over the last ten years. One of the main features of the programme fostered by BIM in the processing sector is the expansion and re-equipment of firms which are embarking on a phased development of their facilities. This will accelerate the movement from primary processed to semi-processed and finished products.

The growth in shore employment has been most marked in the western under-developed regions of the country. These areas have unemployment figures which are among the highest in the Community and fish is one of the few resources available to provide jobs for the people there.

Government policy is to increase employment, both nationally and regionally, and the industry, with the help of BIM, the IDA and Udaras na Gaeltachta is responding to the challenge. Examples of this are the first Irish canning factory located in Donegal in 1977, and the industrial complex at Killybegs, the country's largest port.

Five ports were designated by the Government as major fishery harbour centres, in the mid-1960s, and it has been Government policy to concentrate development at these ports. The ports in question are Killybegs, Rossaveal, Castletownbere, Dunmore East and Howth.

Killybegs, as mentioned above, is the largest fishing port in the country and its development is continuing. An additional IR£1 million has been allocated for the provision of a new auction shed and boat-repair facilities at the port. In addition there are eight processing factories producing everything from fishmeal to packaged fish products for the catering and consumer markets, as well as boat-building, engineering works, net-making and other ancillary industries.

Recently an additional IR£2.5 million, with substantial Irish Government and EEC Aid, has been made available for investment by processors in processing and cold storage to cope with increased landings, especially to facilitate more added value to the mackerel catches.

Over IR£2.5 million has already been spent on the infrastructural facilities at Castletownbere, including the provision of quays, synchrolift and water supply. The State investment in Castletownbere has now resulted in the establishment of the large fish processing plant of Eiranova which will become the catalyst for future projects in the port. Discussions are taking place with other firms for such facilities as fishmeal, cold storage, general fish processing, engineering and boat-repair facilities.

The port facilities at Dunmore East have been completed, while major renovations are well advanced at Howth. A new pier has been completed for the Galway and Aran fleet at Rossaveal, Co. Galway and infrastructural facilities such as an ice plant, auction shed and oil bunkering have already been completed.

Mariculture (fish farming)

BIM operates a Mariculture Grants Scheme and an advisory service geared to the development of fish farming projects. Potential fish farmers can avail of technical, marketing and financial advice under BIM's extension services for mariculture. Grant levels varying from 10% to 30% towards eligible capital expenditure may be given to approved projects with a lower limit of 10% applying in cases where projects are eligible for FEOGA aid. Grant-aid from FEOGA may be up to 50% of capital costs. Pilot projects involving small scale investment will also be grant-aided.

Much interest had developed in mariculture and a number of ventures have been started or are proposed. Last year the value of production was IR£1,500,000 and it is expected that this will rise to IR£2 million this year.

Already there are about 40 fish farms around the Irish coast. They range from major commercial operations to small, pilot projects and they produce salmon, trout, mussels, oysters and scallops. Before the end of the decade, it is reckoned that Irish salmon farms will produce 1,500 tonnes a year — more than double the annual haul today by Irish fishermen. Oyster farming is already well-established in Ireland and some 20 beds are now producing both Atlantic and Pacific oysters for the gourmets of Ireland and Europe. Tralee Bay has the largest natural oyster bed in Europe and this shellfish also grows naturally at Clarinbridge, Kilkerrin, Bertragh Buoy and Aughinish Bay. Seed is also being produced in artificial ponds in a venture by Atlantic Shellfish at Rossmore, Co. Cork where high quality Pacific oysters are also being produced. Today we produce approximately 900 tonnes of oysters and by 1983 the target is 1,500 tonnes.

Mussel culture on the sea bottom as in Wexford, produces large meaty mussels, ideal for processing, pickling or canning. Wexford mussels in a number of forms are now exported to most of the EEC markets.

Rainbow trout have been grown in fresh-water in Ireland for many years and a dozen farms between them produce 400-500 tonnes.

Fish farming is potentially a major arm of the Irish fishing industry but there is no overnight bonanza in the business. It calls for tremendously hard work, dedication and high risk.

Education and training:

BIM has now become the central body for the coordination of all fisheries education and training. Its aim is to provide a higher level of technical competence for seagoing personnel and a career structure for new entrants to the industry.

The National Fishery Training Centre at Greencastle, Co. Donegal, has become the focal point in planning an integrated manpower training policy.

The role of the National Fishery Training Centre has been enlarged through the provision of external courses, which incorporate a Mobile Training Unit. This unit, which was recently commissioned by the Minister for Fisheries, will take training to the fishermen in their home ports. A training vessel will also be provided at the Centre for training in fishing techniques, navigation, and deck safety. Training for existing fishermen, who are presently uncertificated, is being given top priority through the expansion of the existing BIM port courses. All courses now emphasise the practical involvement of the student.

Future growth and prospects

The Council of Ministers of the EEC has declared its intention to apply the

Common Fisheries Policy in such a manner as to ensure the continued and progressive development of the Irish fishing industry on the basis of the Irish Government's Programme for Fisheries Development. It is BIM's policy to promote an environment which will make the achievement of this objective for development possible. This will entail a change of emphasis by the Irish fishing fleet from a pattern of fishing for herring to one of fishing for white fish and other species. Over the past number of years herring has been the dominant species in Irish landings, but because of overfishing usually by other fleets, the available quantity of herring has fallen dramatically.

There is considerable scope for the further development of the processing industry and thus the creation of many more, much needed jobs on shore in the handling, treatment and packing of fish and fish products at the country's major fishing ports.

In order to realise the full potential of this development it is essential that the quantity of commercially valuable fish be landed on an increasing and reasonably continuous basis, and that cost structures here remain in line so as to enable Irish fish products to compete effectively in world markets.

Time, and hard economic facts, are on the fishing industry's side. Many fishing vessels from Germany, France, Holland, Belgium and Britain at present fish on grounds off the west, north-west and south-west coasts. With the increasing cost of fuel, not to mention its scarcity value, it is going to make far more economic sense to land the fish at a nearby Irish port, process it there and transport the final product to markets on the European mainland.

As mentioned previously, there is a trend for firms to move from the processing of simply bulk products to more sophisticated production. BIM's market and investment development strategies are aimed at accelerating this trend. In addition, the Board is promoting the establishment of facilities to cater for the processing of the under-utilised species such as mackerel and sprat. The provision of these facilities is being programmed alongside the establishment of an increased and suitable catching potential. Likewise facilities for processing increasing quantities of white fish are being encouraged, e.g. dried and smoked products.

Joint venture projects between Irish and European partners are being fostered to harness the potential for employment creating added-value production and integrated processing/catching operations involving Irish processing facilities and foreign technical and marketing expertise.

The EEC programme for the regulation of fisheries within the Community for the seas around Ireland is based on a system of quotas, together with fishing plans for the various national fleets. However, fisheries negotiations at Brussels have not yet been completed and a definitive policy on fishery conservation and management has yet to be agreed between the ten for future years. Because of this uncertainty, it is difficult to forecast the future exactly except to say that it will be one of growth.

Index